With an Adamantine Sickle

A Devotional to the Titans

Edited by Rebecca Buchanan

❖ 1 ❖

<u>Dedication</u>

To the forgotten Powers,
The primal spirits of sun and moon and star,
Mountain and river and sea,
Time and the seasons

We sing your names again

Introduction

The Titans — individually and collectively — are an enigma. Who are they? Which aspects of creation do they guard or represent? How were they honored by the ancient Greeks, if they were honored at all? How are they honored by contemporary polytheists, if at all? And what, exactly, *is* a Titan?

Broadly defined, the Titans are the elder generation of Hellenic Deities and their immediate offspring. And sometimes their grandchildren, as well. Though sometimes their grandchildren are counted among the Olympian generation who eventually supplanted the Titans as the ruling Deities. The distinction between Titan and Olympian is as much political as it is generational.

It's all a bit murky.

Consider Hekate. Traditionally the Titan-Goddess of magic and witchcraft, she is explicitly honored by Zeus in the pages of Hesiod's *Theogony,* and was actively worshipped up through the rise of Christianity. Today, she is one of the most popular Deities in Goddess Spirituality, Wicca, Hellenismos, Religio (Roman polytheism), and witchcraft.

Then there are Rhea and Kronos. Often equated with the Anatolian Goddess Kybele, Rhea was the original Queen, the sister-wife of Kronos. She sided with her children in their war against her husband, and helped place Zeus on the throne of Olympus. Though supplanted as Queen by her own daughter, Hera, she maintained a well-respected position as a Goddess of agriculture, mountains, cities, and ecstatic mystery traditions. Today, she is known, if not widely honored.

Kronos, on the other hand, has a more complicated history. Variously portrayed as a cannibalistic tyrant and as the ruler of a golden age of innocence and prosperity, he castrated his own father Ouranos to assume rulership of creation. He was then overthrown in turn by Zeus, who cast him into the deepest pit of Tartaros. In some stories, he remains there still; in others, he was eventually released by Zeus and given guardianship of the Blessed Isles in Elysium. If he is honored at all today, it is usually in his role as husband of Rhea or as a Deity of agriculture.

And so it went. Various Titans retained nominal positions of authority in the new order. Others were cast aside, cast down, or so completely forgotten that only their names and the barest of information remains. Some of the Titans acquired damaging reputations with the passage of time, thus further justifying their overthrow by the younger Olympians.

And so we find ourselves here, with a devotional in honor of the Titans. Why? Well, most simply, these Powers may be largely forgotten, but they are still worthy of due respect and honor. They are Powers, greater than us, more intimately connected to and responsible for the workings of creation.

Secondly, there is the politics of those old myths. The victors tell the tales, and all that. Such stories are only a fraction of the spirituality that was lived and practiced in ancient Greece, and that is lived and practiced by Hellenic polytheists today. In other words, there is more to the Titans than a few passages in the few surviving stories that have been told and retold and translated and transcribed across the millennia. The contributors to this anthology, through research and personal gnosis, hope to bring those lost elements back into the light.

Third, to our knowledge, no such other text exists. Yes, there are plenty of contemporary devotional works written in honor of Hekate. There are even a few for Rhea-Kybele. But there are none to the Titans collectively.

Within these pages, you will find poems and hymns, meditations and rites, artwork and essays and fiction. The anthology is divided into four sections, each loosely organized by the type of Titan being honored. The first is dedicated to "The God of the Sickle and the Great Mother," i.e. Kronos and Rhea. It also includes a few pieces to little-known Titans such as Dione, and to the Titans as a family.

The second section, "The Heavens and the Deep," is an offering to the Titans associated with the sun, moon, stars, sea, and world-ocean. Here, you will find poems and fiction about Ouranos, Okeanos, Atlas, Kreios, Hyperion, Helios, Selene, and Leto.

The third section, "Memory, Intellect, and Time," is more varied. There are poems, short stories, and essays here about Lethe (forgetfulness), Mnemosyne (memory), Metis (wisdom), Iapetos, Prometheus, Koios, Themis, and Phoebe.

The fourth section, dedicated to "The Underworld," is focused almost exclusively on Hekate. This should probably not come as a surprise. She is the Titan with the clearest connection to the afterlife.

Finally, the first appendix contains an alphabetical listing of most of the Titans, with brief descriptions of their areas of responsibility and their family lineages. We recommend that readers peruse that section first, then dive into the body of the anthology.

This devotional has been a labor of love for many of its contributors. It has been a long time in coming, and we hope that it will inspire polytheists everywhere to take a closer look at these Forgotten Powers.

Rebecca Buchanan
Editor-in-Chief, Spring 2022

Table of Contents

<u>The Heavens and the Deep</u>

<u>Memory, Intellect, and Time</u>

The Underworld

The God of the Sickle
and the Great Mother

❖ 15 ❖

Abundatia by Peter Paul Rubens

<u>Beneath an Adamantine Sickle</u>

by J.K. Bywaters

When I first returned to the Commonwealth of Virginia after four years of undergraduate studies in New England, there were an even one hundred wineries in the Old Dominion. Now, nearly twenty-one years on, there are more than three times that number. Perhaps it is silly, but I am proud of them. I think that the viticulturists and vintners in Virginia are doing some good work, and some creative work. It is a pleasure to see. (And, after the national ban on glyphosate finally went into effect in January 2022, all of the wine, happily, is safe to drink.) I will admit that I myself have never pressed so much as a single grape for any of the commercial vineyards in the Commonwealth, nor seen through to maturation a single cask's worth of wine, but I am proud of the wineries nonetheless. I think that their work reflects positively on the Commonwealth, and in some subconscious fashion, as I myself am a native and sometimes resident, I suppose that I fancy that it must also reflect positively on me by association. It's the same sort of silly pride that I feel when the New England Patriots win the Super Bowl. I've never put on pads for the team, and coach Belichick has never once taken instruction from me, not that he needs it. But still, I am proud of my home-away-from-home team.

Sometimes, for a lark, I like to go for an amble through the Virginia countryside with the casual sort of intention of finding some vineyard which I haven't yet seen. I avoid the sprawling suburbs and continuous strip malls of northern Virginia, all of it one miasmic suburb of Washington, DC, and I avoid the sprawling military and industrial port cities to the southeast, but that still leaves me the Eastern Shore, the Middle Peninsula, the Northern Neck, almost the entire Piedmont, the Shenandoah, and the Ridge and Valley region, including the whole southwestern panhandle. Depending on where I travel, I am more likely to find soybeans, feed corn, winter wheat, hay (chiefly timothy), or even tobacco, but grapes are on the upswing, and more and more vineyards are popping up. The peanut used to be Virginia's cash crop, and the state now produces more grapes than goobers. I keep a Rand McNally road atlas tucked under the seat, and have two maps in my glove compartment — one being a roadmap of Virginia, the second being a map published by the Virginia Wine Marketing Office, and both of them more than twenty years old themselves — but I never use them for direction. I follow my intuition, when I have one, and other times, I follow my whimsy.

I find that, for the most part, I have tended to turn up in the places where I am meant to be.

Once, of an afternoon in the springtime of this year, I set out from my family's old cottage on the banks of the mighty Rappahannock River. I ambled north on US 17, turned west on Virginia route 3, and southwest on the great US 29. I found that I was developing an offhanded sort of opinion that the thing to do would be to follow 29 to nearly the very southern edge of the state, then pick up US 360 east and eventually northeast, all the way back to 17 again. I had no set impression regarding how long this would take, but as it was already past three o'clock, it seemed to me that I was in for at least another day of it. That was fine. I had stopped at a number of points of interest, and thought that I might could get in one more before looking for a place to roost for the evening.

Virginia, incidentally, has an uncommonly high number of interestingly-named little towns or regions. I don't use the maps to tell me how to get to any point in particular, but, when I end up there, it is of passing interest to know where I am, and the maps are good for that much. On today's trip, as it fell out, I had passed close by both Chance and Hustle on 17. Once I turned into the west, the names of the little districts tended to get wilder. There was Wilderness, Locust Grove, and Lake of the Woods. Now, off of 29, I found myself near an area apparently called Brightwood — a name that I loved. Nearby on the map, I could see Wolftown, Radiant, Oak Park, Miles Cross, and Woodberry

Forest, but of particular interest to me was a place that showed up on the maps as Zeus. That seemed auspicious, somehow. The name sounded like a portent, to me. I had a deep-rooted suspicion that it was likely that there were grapes being grown and put to use in the area. I made an exception to my casual practice of not using the maps for advance directions, and I set out to see what Zeus had in store for me.

I made a soft right off of 29 at a fork, driving into woods on both sides of the narrow two-lane road. In less than a mile, there was another fork, with another soft right hand turn, and I took it. I had traveled only another half-mile before I was rewarded with rows of old vines only a short distance off the road to the northeast. There were acres of grapes. I slowed, looking for a signpost, or a point of entry. After several hundred yards, I saw it, once again off the road to my right. Two marble pillars rose perhaps twelve feet into the air, with Corinthian capitals, vertical volutes, and foliate detail. Between them there lay a heavy marble arch. Along this arch were incised a single row of Greek letters beneath an adamantine sickle that looked to be chiseled from quartz. The letters read

Κρόνος

and I read the letters. It is a peculiarity of my university to require of all incoming students, whether matriculating freshmen or transfers, a semester's study in Greek classics, philosophy, rhetoric, oratory, history, and linguistics.

"*Cronus*," I said aloud, and smiled.

Some of the wineries in Virginia think highly of themselves, and have fine dining establishments and polo fields on their grounds. Others are modest affairs run out of a basement room in a quiet subdivision, labors of love by home winemakers who have acquired a license to sell commercially, in whatever small quantity that they may. As such, I have driven down winery roads paved with asphalt, gravel roads, and dirt roads. I have driven down roads of macadam, and, near the rivers and the bay, roads of crushed oyster shell. But this was the first time in my recollection that I had ever turned onto a winery road comprised of evenly-spaced, regularly-cut, smooth and rectangular pavers of stone. To the east, the acres of old vines. To the west, woods. Ahead of me, a slight rise in the terrain, and from only a short distance beyond a little hilltop, a plume of smoke rose into the air. I crested the hilltop and slowed to a stop some fifty yards beyond it. Another fifty yards beyond where I stopped, the road came to an end at what appeared to be a small open-air temple of Hellenic design, crafted of stone pillars of a similar fashion to the propylon a short ways back. There was a roof, which was no more than twelve feet high, but the actual walls were perhaps only three feet high; atop them were set the pillars, evenly-spaced from one side to the next, so that it was possible to look from one side of the structure straight through it and out again on the opposite side. From the south, I could look through to the north and see the woods beyond, and the mountains rising above them. To the left of this temple structure, and only a little ways beyond the point at which the road came to its end, a giant of a man was hauling dry vines, brush, and brambles to a small burn pile. Although each of my nephews has had the temerity to grow taller than me, and my own grandfather stood at 6' 5" during an era when such a thing was generally not done, I am not a small man. I stand 6' 3" myself, but I could see that the man ahead of me had me by at least six inches. He was bare to the waist, wearing only what looked to be linen breeches, and thin-soled sandals. He was powerfully built, though not bulky, and to my surprise seemed to be at least seventy years of age, judging by his lined features and by his hair and beard, which were the color of ash. Something — I could not tell what — swung heavily from his neck. At first I took it to be a leather pouch of some kind, a medicine bag or some such. He was in the act of moving from the edge of the woods toward the burn pile when first I saw him. In his right hand he dragged a thick growth of vine along behind him through ankle-high grasses, and in his left hand he carried a sickle, apparently sized for his own use, though itself but a miniature version of the one that crowned the propylon. I could see it, glimmering in the light of the late afternoon, each time his left hand swung forward to oppose the long stride of his right leg. He turned suddenly, first only his head but immediately following with his body, and stood facing me as I gripped the wheel, watching. In that moment, for an instant, I thought that I was surely trespassing, that, vines or not, I had surely driven onto someone's private land. I was not welcome here. I raised my right hand to him, briefly, and dropped it on to the gear lever, intending to put the vehicle in reverse and back down the road. But before my hand came to rest on the knob, he pointed at me with the top, outer curve of the sickle, then threw his arm wide from his body in a gesture of opening, indicating the stone structure.

He was directing me where to park.

I pulled up to the front of the structure where the road gave out. There was room for perhaps six cars if all were nestled together. As I stepped out and moved to close the door behind me, he strode from around the corner. He was even taller than I had first taken him to be; had he worn thick-soled work boots instead of the sandals, he would have stood better than 7' tall. His eyes were the color of flint, and looked to be as hard. His hair and beard were not only the color of ash, but had ash *in* them, no doubt from his fire. His belly, chest, and shoulders all heaved. His nostrils flared with his breath, but he did not pant. He had thrown down the vines, but still carried the sickle in his left hand. I could see now that what he wore around his neck was no pouch at all, but a hard stone that would have filled my cupped hand. It hung from a thin chain of some white metal by two thin pegs set one on either side of the stone. Before I could speak, a stocky youth came around the corner after him, baring a woven basket with a few white towels. He was young, not yet twenty-five by my best guess, but he had a thick dark beard, and coarse dark hair spilling out from under a large white flop hat. He had a strange gait — not exactly a limp, but something like it. He was perhaps 5' tall, and his short stature was emphasized by the older man towering over him. Without looking, the older man took a towel, wrung it out, and wiped his brow, his neck, his chest. He let it fall beside him into the grass, and took a second. With this one he completed his toilette by wiping the underside of each arm, from wrist to axilla, then over the curve of his ribs to his hip. He let fall the second towel. The youth regarded him with something like love, or reverence, and did not divert his eyes from the older man until, for the second time, this individual jabbed at me with the top of his sickle.

"Férte mia petséta ston xéno."

At this, the younger man turned and came to me, proffering his basket. I took a towel, wonderfully cold and refreshing, and wiped my face with it. I folded it and handed it back to the younger man. He took it. He turned then at his heel and made to retrieve the two towels dropped by the giant. This done, he disappeared back around the corner again. For the third time, the man jabbed at me with the back of his blade. For the second time, he swung his arm outward, in a sweep towards the edifice. For the first time, I saw him smile.

"Come," he said. "*Wine.*"

We came in through an opening in the low wall just in front of where I had parked. He walked before me, and, although even his formidable height still permitted him a grace of more than three feet before the ceiling, I saw him duck under the intavolatura, as a man will when he is used to hitting his head. Inside, the space was sparse and simply furnished: four small round wooden tables, each with two chairs, and, complementing the surrounding stone columns, a freestanding plinth set a few feet out from the center of the back wall. He waved his sickle at a table. I sat. He walked behind the stone slab and produced two bottles from a low wooden rack. He set them atop the plinth, lifting them both up between the fingers of his right hand, and at once he performed the most offhandedly brutal act of sabrage I have ever witnessed before or since, sweeping the necks from both bottles at once, not with the back of the sickle but with its edge. The necks fell with a conjoined clink onto the stone, each describing an opposing circle on its surface until the lips touched in a kiss made of glass. The titan snatched the bottles up again in the same one-handed grip, and came around from the bar to join me at the table. The bottles were of a thick, opaque, green glass, and unlabeled. He sat heavily down on the chair across from me, let the sickle fall at his feet, and took one of the bottles in his left hand. He held out the bottle that remained in his right hand to me. I took it. He raised the bottle in his left.

"*Na zíseis!*" he said. (*"May you live;"* my favorite toast, as it happens.)

We drank.

I remembered enough to offer in return "*Boreís na zíseis gia pánta, kai na psofisei o Haros."* (*"May you live forever, and may Charon drop dead."*) This made him smile.

We drank again.

This, though, was pushing the envelope of my out-of-practice, twenty-years-gone Greek pleasantries. With some embarrassment, and some regret, I switched to English.

"This wine is exquisite. I've never tasted anything like it anywhere in Virginia; anywhere at all, in fact. What is it? A blend, or a single varietal?"

He understood me perfectly. "This is a Liatiko," he replied. "It was once cultivated exclusively in Crete. These — " he nodded his great head at the vines "— are the first vines taken off the island, so far as we know. So far as it matters." He shrugged, and drank. "We grow the old world varietals — *very* old world. Liatiko, Dafni, Agiorgitiko, Kidonitsa. Xinomavro. A few others. You would have to ask my grandson. Dio. He is the winemaker. All this — ” he raised a hand, almost awkwardly, as if not used to making reference to anything without the sickle in his hand “— is still new to me. I am old. I am old, very old, but still I see new things. Still things amaze me. Delight me. Still, I am learning.” He closed his hand over the stone around his neck and made as if to massage it. He grimaced at the vines.

“What is that stone?” I asked him. “Did you find it here, on the land?”

He drank, and I drank with him.

Behind my host, in back of the temple, I saw a young man, fair of face, ride into view from the west, from the direction of the woods. He had bits of leaf and vine in his hair. I could see that he wore a loose and billowing shirt that was white, or nearly so, but torn in places, and all over stained with purple and russet. He was astride the largest goat I had ever seen.

“I killed my father,” said the old man.

I coughed, lurched forward in the chair, choked on the wine. The young man glanced in at our little tableau, and before my own eyes squeezed shut against the acidic burn of the wine in my sinuses, I saw his eyes widen. He was off the goat and vaulting over the low wall at the temple’s rear, and hurrying around the plinth toward us. His shirt, unbuttoned, swung open as he moved, and through my watering eyes I saw that his skin, too, was cut, scabbed, and blotchy with stains from the grapes.

"Pappouli!" cried the young man. "What happened? What have you done?" I heard this as I opened my watering eyes, catching my breath, sputtering. Close up, the young man looked to be of an age with the towel bearer, but with a look both more regal and more wild. His grandfather glanced at him, then met my eyes again before allowing himself to be urged up and onto his feet. His grandson must have stood nearly 6' tall himself, but the older man made the younger look diminutive. The younger man clapped his grandfather on the back, squeezed his shoulder, and, to my further surprise, pat several times the stone that lay on the old man's chest.

"Go back to your cutting. I will tarry here with our guest." The titan said nothing, but he touched his grandson's face in passing, and he stepped easily over the back wall of the structure, once more ducking his head. The young man picked up the bottle in front of me and examined it. It was almost full, but he, leaning close to me and lowering his voice as if in confidence, told me "you will want more." He stood taller, and pursed his lips. "*I* will want more, surely." In a moment he was back behind the great stone slab. He produced two more bottles, and then, after a moment's consideration, two more. He returned to the table, where he almost collapsed into the chair opposite me in the same heavy flop as the old man. I had not noticed even a corkscrew, much less a sickle, but I saw that he had somehow gotten two of the bottles open.

"This," he said, pausing to drink, ". . . is the Kidonitsa. If there is anyone else growing this grape in the Commonwealth or on the entire eastern seaboard, I do not know of it. It is the wine of Sparta. Drink, friend. It tastes of quince preserves. It tastes of the autumn remembering the summer."

We drank. We paused together, for a moment, and he eyed me in a way that seemed to be appraising, or shrewd, or apologetic, or all of these qualities together.

"My grandfather and I have not always had a good relationship," he said. "He used to be afraid of me. He was afraid of me before I was born. For the first time, I mean." He shook his head. "I have another birth day every year." He shrugged. "I am Dio. My grandfather is Cronus. It was my idea to make wine, but he taught me everything about the harvest that I know."

"You named the winery for him."

"Yes. This was to help him with his madness." He raised his hands, palms up, a *what can you do?* "He is mad, you know. In his way. You must have seen more than a hint of it. I hope that he did not upset you too badly." He sighed. "It was his own father who brought out the madness in him.

His father was afraid of his children. He did not understand them; he did not know them, not truly, and he feared them. So, he taught them fear. He kept my grandfather locked up, along with all of his brothers and sisters. In so doing, he taught them fear twice over. In the case of my grandfather, Cronus, three times — for my grandfather, too, feared his children. Most of all, he feared my father." I watched the young man as he paused to drink again. He seemed at his ease, even while talking with me, a stranger, so freely. Paradoxically, he seemed amused, even entertained by his own confessional.

"Cronus saw himself in my father. My father was called Deuce, because he was like a second coming of his own father. Of course, that is not his real name." He winked at me. "I know what you are thinking, my friend. *Why does he tell me these things? Has he no shame for his family?* Ha!" He gave a sudden cry, wild and shrill; it sounded like *Euoi!* It sat me up in my chair.

"No," he said, smiling happily.

"No?" I had lost the thread.

"No!" cried he, with a congenial sound. "First, friend, you are no stranger to me. In fact, my family likes to tell me that I have never met a stranger. Certainly no one stranger than myself. And after all, I am a stranger in this land. A foreigner." He crossed his arms on the table before him, and raised his brows. "And I guess that I look the part. Secondly, no, I am not ashamed of madness. I do not fear it. Why should I? Why should *you*?" He paused to consider the wine. "Also — " He sipped. "You know," he said, "My grandfather didn't kill my father. They *tried* to kill each other, yes, many times, in truth, but my father is still with us. Figuratively. He lives up on the mountain."

"He didn't say that he'd killed *your* father," I interjected. "He said that he'd killed his own."

The young man snorted; he almost guffawed.

"O, well, yes. He did kill his own father. In a manner of speaking, yes." He paused. "That was ages ago, though. I wonder what made him think of that?" He drank again, and realization illuminated his features. He smiled, and raised an index finger in the air. "The stone. You said something to him about the stone, yes? Or he saw you looking at it, perhaps?"

"Yes."

"He *ate* that stone, you know. Actually swallowed it whole. And not even because of anything like a wager that he had made, or a challenge that someone set for him. Just pure compulsion. Thought that he *had to* do it." He shook his head, remembering an old exasperation that has settled into a sort of inconsequential mystification. "He finds it uncomfortable to talk about, and I don't press him on the point, but I believe that he wears the stone around his neck like that as a constant reminder." He drank, stuck his nose over the lip of the bottle, sniffed deeply, and drank again. "Or as a penance. That could be. I am sure that he feels a little foolish for having eaten such a great rock, you know." He drank. "But I have no doubt whatsoever that he would do it again, if presented with the same set of circumstances." He looked at me with a smile that was both genuine and indecipherable. "Madness — " He broke off, tilted back the bottle, tilted back his head, tilted back in his chair. He finished its contents. He drew the back of his hand across his mouth. He smacked his lips. He regarded the other bottles there on our table for a moment, then seemed to be surprised to see me when he looked up from his moment's fancy.

"Madness has always run the men of my family. I do not mean only to say that it has run *in* the men of my family, that is, that it has been a genetic trait in the male line, though certainly this is true. We are very much all mad here. My great-grandfather did not understand it. My grandfather was afraid of it. My father was enraged by it. All of them, at times, have been ruled by it. And — " He took up a new bottle, and drank. "I am ruled by it." He drank again. "I myself am ruled by it, this madness. Perhaps the madness comes from my forefathers, or perhaps the madness was delivered to each of us in turn by this world. It is, wonderfully, a mad world." He raised the bottle to his lips. His continual libation punctuated his thoughts. To my surprise, I found that I had almost come to the bottom of the bottle of Kidonitsa. I remembered the still nearly full bottle of Liatiko that this young man's grandfather had sabered and given to me. My young host took a long, slow, deep breath.

"Ah — Liatiko. It is a wonderful wine, yes, and one of my grandfather's favorites. It reminds him of beautiful things. And I believe that it helps him to be comfortable with his madness." Again, he drank. "This is what I have tried to do." He smiled benevolently. His eyes gleamed. He looked all around him, even turning in his chair to look over his shoulder. He raised his arms in the air as if he would walk into a lover's embrace.

"To be comfortable with madness. To embrace madness. To relish and savor the mad, the unusual, the wild and raving, the coarse and vulgar, the bestial. To recognize the absurdity in the terrifying, and the utter foolishness of the tragic. To allow this madness to ferment and to refine itself into merriment. And to help others to see that this is possible. Perhaps it is as . . ." He broke off for a moment, considering. ". . . *nice*. Perhaps it is as *nice* for others to see this truth as I have found it to be. For myself — " He drank deeply. "— I find the truth of this both comforting and enlivening. It is, as we all know, a mad world. Yes. Incidentally — " He drank, and I, in agreement, drank with him, finishing the Kidonitsa. It really did taste of quince preserves.

"— if there is ever a time when someone has you at a loss for something to say — if you are ever stymied in your conversation — you can always say to them *'it is a mad world.'* It is always true, always appropriate, always relevant." Again, he seemed to consider for a moment. "And, perhaps it is also true to say that it is always *reverent* to say this. Yes, yes, reverent as well as relevant. If the gods are mad themselves, then whether the madness is inherent to their bodies or instead it came into them from the world, then to acknowledge the madness of the world is a sort of psalm, I think."

There was a rough and casual clopping of hooves behind me, and as I turned, the great Boer goat strode into the temple. It passed close beside me and came to a stop facing Dio. It tossed its head, ruddy beard flying, and blew an abrupt burst of air through its nose and closed lips, a queer sort of half sneeze, half snort. It sounded like nothing as much as though the great beast was scoffing at Dio's words. I watched him drag his hand through his thick curly hair and pull out one of the grape leaves stuck in it. He put it into the goat's mouth. Satisfied, the goat continued to the back of the room, where it reared up onto its hind legs and put its front hooves on the low stone wall. It began to whet its horns on one of the columns. Dio, who had turned to watch the goat go on its way with evident amusement, turned back to me and shook his head.

"Madness," he repeated. "We live our lives between earth and sky. We grow up from the earth; we grow, always, toward the sky. The earth gives us sustenance; the sky gives us inspiration. We grow full. We grow stronger. We grow rich. And life — " He hooked a finger as if beckoning someone to come, but turned it on its side and sliced it through the air between us. "— it cuts us down. It cuts us off at the knees, or the sex, or the belly, or the nape of the neck. We fall. We fall beneath the sickle." He pushed back from the table, again tilted back in his chair, and again put his palms in the air, asking me and the world at large *what am I to do?* He took a deep breath. He let fall his chair behind him as he jumped to his feet and threw both hands into the air over his head. Again came the wild cry of *Euoi!* Then he leaned over the table and fair bellowed at me, with wild eyes and the winedark spit flying from his lips.

"We rise! We live! We live again. Life cannot kill us. Only death can do that." He almost sat, stopped himself, turned, and righted his chair. With a pirouette, and a mock bow to the chair, he turned and once more flopped heavily into it.

"Life can only drive you mad. And only then if you let it. And so, I think, *why not let it?* Why not go as mad as life is itself, right along with it? If we do this — if we celebrate our madness — are we not celebrating the madness of life? Are we not celebrating life itself? And can we be said to be *alive*, that is, to be living, really living, if we are not celebrating? This is why I honor the madness of my family. This is why I make wine, why I drink it, why I give freely to others. It is why I have been a foreigner in many lands. It is why I preach the gospel of this madness, and of madness transformed into wild joy: *because this is the essence of life!*"

I was on my feet, both on them and off of them, because I found that I was jumping up and down, sloshing the bottle of Liatiko and cheering, laughing, crying. My young host laughed, nodded, then flopped his hand at me, a *go on* gesture.

"I say nothing to you that you do not know to be true yourself, and no knowledge of this truth comes to you by any other means than your own body, your own body alive and in this mad world, this beautiful and terrifying world." He stood again, and I found myself coming around the table to meet him as he moved to embrace me. He pulled me down by either side of my face and gave me a rough kiss on the forehead.

"This is my gift to you — this, and wine." He put one of the bottles from the table in my hand. "You cannot see it from here, but there is a path just there, at the edge of the wood. Follow the path for but a short distance and you'll come to a small cottage. There is a bed, there is cool water to drink, there are all of the sounds of the night advancing toward us. Someone will bring you a plate of food — olives, good white bread, a little fruit. You have had a bit of wine with us this evening, my friend. Stay on." He looked back at the table, and picked up a bottle. He raised it to me, then raised it above his head. I followed his hand with my eyes and saw that the ceiling was more vaulted than I had thought; especially with the light beginning to fade, there looked to be near infinite space above the lip of the bottle. He pulled it back to himself and had a brief, rough sip. He put the bottle into my hand.

"Last sip. And the last sip is lucky. I have heard it said that there is an idea in the last sip. No, no —" He gripped my wrist as I made to raise the bottle. "Take it with you to the cottage. Perhaps you remember these words? If not, I will help you remember. I will bring them back to you." With his hands over mine, he raised the bottle between us.

"*Gia tin zoí! Gia tin tréla! Gia tin ékstasi!*" He smiled up at me. "Yes? *'For life. For madness. For ecstasy.'* Yes." He put an arm around me and led me to the back; he meant for us to go over the wall, and we did. I wondered, in passing, where the great goat had gone. The feel of the ivy under my hands, the sound of my feet coming down on the earth, the scent of the lingering smoke from the fire of Cronus — all of these delighted me.

"Say a prayer for Cronus," he said. "Say a prayer for my grandfather's comfort, and for his madness. And this for us all. This for our world. And rise! And live!"

He hurried off, back around the building toward the front. I walked into the woods.

***

In the night, in the little cottage, I heard the cries of *Euoi!* that rang through the wood, through the world, between the earth and the sky, and I found that I was on my feet, and knew not if the cries were my hosts' or were my own.

Homer's Island

by Sophia Kouidou-Giles

Women's voices echo
Off cobblestone narrows and
Castle village walls.
Tales of stranded sailors,
Sea monsters and heroes
Slip into dreams seeking answers.

The ancient poet perches
Settled on his wide rock throne.
He leads his faithful followers
Into the cadence of epic.
Below him whispers drift
From Cybele's pagan shrine
Stirring his soul with inspiration.

In the valley, after sunset,
An ancient spirit, vibrant and revealing,
Slithers in my room and
Whispers of ancestral sacrifices.

In stillness, devoutly I listen
To echoes of the Goddess in Homer's Chios,
A patch of fragrant rock
Sown in the Aegean.

<u>Hymn to Cronos</u>

by ϪΙΜΟΥϹ

Hail, Sickle Bearing Cronos,
Father of the gods,
Lord of the harvest,
Bringer of good fortune,
Ruler of Elysium,
And creator of man.
I thank and praise you on this day,
Bless my life and grant good fortune.

<u>Hymn to the Great Mother Rhea-Kybele</u>
by Robin Wilcox

Divine Mother, hear our prayer:
Grant our loved ones health and prosperity!
Great Goddess, wife and parent of Father Zeus,
Let us lay our problems at Your immovable feet.
Please come whenever we call, Queen of
        wild beasts.
Companion of Bakkhos, lover of Áttis,
Source of immortal Gods and mortals, too,
Shower us in Your blessings and take us into Your
        invincible hands.
Highest of Goddesses, in You we are given life.
Ruler Whose Hand is Above, giver of goodly gifts,
Consort of Earth-Shaking Poseidon,
Smile upon us, and close our lives in peace.

Kronos and Rhea in Pythagoreanism

by John Opsopaus, PhD

In this chapter I explore how Kronos and Rhea are understood in Pythagoreanism, a spiritual tradition that has been practiced continuously, in one form or another, for at least twenty-six centuries. According to ancient Greek tradition, Pythagoras (572–497 BCE) studied with the Egyptians, Phoenicians, Chaldeans, Brahmans, and Zoroastrians, and was initiated into all their mysteries. He is supposed to have met with Zoroaster (Zarathustra), but scholars believe that Zoroaster lived in the second millennium BCE, and so it is likely that the Greek tradition reflects a meeting between Pythagoras and Zoroastrian Magi. In any case, there are many traces of Zoroastrianism in Pythagorean philosophy. In particular, there are similarities between the central duality of Pythagoreanism and the dual gods of Zoroaster (Ahura-Mazda and Ahriman). However, there are also connections to Zurvanism, a Zoroastrian "heresy," which placed a primordial god Zurvân Akarana (Infinite Time) before the dual gods. Pythagoras may have learned these ideas from his teacher Pherecydes (fl. 544 BCE), whose cosmology begins with Aiôn (Eternity), the god who engenders the primal duality (discussed below). Pherecydes' book, which is reputed to be the first book of philosophy to have been written in prose, survives in fragments and is a useful source for reconstructing the early Pythagorean system.

Theogony

Before discussing Kronos and Rhea in Pythagoreanism, it will be helpful to start by placing them in context with a brief overview of Pythagorean cosmology. However, I must begin with a warning. Over these two and one-half millennia, Pythagoreans, Platonists, Neopythagoreans, and Neoplatonists have differed among themselves on many technical points of theology, but I will be ignoring these differences, and presenting something like a synthesis of the doctrines. This may seem somewhat intellectually sloppy, but in fact I think it is a mistake to over-emphasize dogmatic details in a religion that is fundamentally mystical. In the end, we come to understand the gods by interacting with them through theurgy.

We will face one of these issues right off, for the best way to understand the cosmology is through theogony, or the birth of the gods. But Pythagoreans disagree as to whether this is to be understood as a historical process, which took place at some point in time, or whether it is a timeless process of emanation. Although I incline to the emanationist view, I will present it as a myth of origins, since I think it is easier to understand that way; in fact the two views are difficult to separate, because we must deal with the birth of Time (*Khronos*) itself. For this reason, I will tell myths in the present tense, which you may interpret as the eternal present or the historical present, as you like.

The myth begins with a primordial unity, a bisexual deity, who is sometimes called Aiôn (Eternity). In fact, this mysterious deity is outside of time and transcends all dualities (even being and non-being, existence and non-existence); therefore Pythagoreans call it the Ineffable Unity (to Arrhêton Hen). Heraclitus (fl. 500 BCE) says, "God is day night, summer winter, war peace, glut hunger (all the opposites, that is the meaning)" (fr. 67). Because it unifies everything, including all the opposites, Unity is paradoxical and contradictory, and the ancients called it ineffable, invisible, unspeakable, unnamable, and unknown; we cannot understand it by logic or describe it in words; we grasp it only insofar as we unite with it.

By self-fertilization Aiôn gives birth to, or divides into, two gods, the first polarity. These gods, who will become the mother and father of the other gods, we call Kronos and Rhea; they govern the primary dualities, including unity/multiplicity, limit/ unlimited, stability/change, form/matter, father/ mother, and male/female. (The latter are polar Platonic Ideas, which are independent of non-binary genders here on earth.) Like *aum*, Aiôn (Aἰών) is a sacred sound composed of vowels (ΑΙΩ) fading into nasalization: pure vibration entering manifestation. ΑΙΩ are the first, middle, and last of the seven Greek vowels (ΑΕΗΙΟΥΩ), corresponding to the Moon, the Sun, and Saturn. The trigraph ΑΙΩ symbolizes the divine polarity and the primordial unity that unites them (also embodied in the sacred name ΙΑΩ, Iaô, which we find in the Greek Magical Papyri).

Kronos and Rhea mate, a "re-union" of the opposites, and thereby become the father and mother of the gods. We will see that Kronos is the Monad (the singular principle) and Rhea is the Indefinite Dyad (the plural principle), and so the union of the two engenders a plurality of divine unities (henads): the gods. Thus they create the empyrean realm, the world of the Olympian gods.

First created are the regents of the second rank of gods, Zeus and Hera; Kronos and Rhea either give birth to them or by their union transform into them; the two processes are hardly different, for gods give birth by creating images of themselves. Next Zeus and Hera create the aetherial realm in which dwell the immortal celestial beings: the gods of the stars and planets. Zeus and Hera are the Craftsman (*Dêmiourgos*) and the Nurse (*Tithênê*), who together create the material realm. Zeus thinks the world-defining Platonic Ideas, which he throws like lightening bolts into the womb of Hera, who nourishes them with her substance, thereby giving birth to our world. Thus she is the life-conferring World Soul (*hê tou Pantos Psychê*, the Soul of The All), who unites the Ideas with matter. So much for now on the genealogy of the gods.

The Monad and the Indefinite Dyad

Pythagoreans explain the gods through the esoteric meaning of the numbers. In particular, they identify Kronos with the Monad (the number One) and Rhea with the Dyad (the number Two). The Monad is relatively easy to understand: he is the principle of unity and constancy. The Dyad, however, is more complex. First, she is the other; if there were only the Monad, there would be no other; thus she causes differentiation and separation. Therefore, Syrianus (fl. 431 CE) identified the Monad and the Dyad with Love (*Philia*) and Strife (*Neikos*), the two principal forces in the universe according to Empedocles (c.495–435 BCE): Love draws together, Strife drives apart (for more on them, see "Fire" in Opsopaus, "Anc. Grk. Eso. Doc. Elem."). Without both identity and differentiation there would be no structure or organization in the cosmos; it would be chaos or a featureless blob.

Pythagoreans explain emanation at all the levels of being between Unity and Matter in terms of three phases: abiding (*monê*) — proceeding (*proödos*) — reverting (*epistrophê*), which explain how an essence can emanate into more substantial forms and yet retain its identity. The essence, or unchanging nature, of a thing is abiding or remaining; it is the male axis. Yet it has the power or potential (*dynamis*) to relate to other things, to proceed by a continuous flux toward greater "participation," that is, toward more substantial embodiment, the direction of greater multiplicity; this is the female axis. However, this flowing forth would cause it to lose its definition, so it reverts or turns back toward its origin so that it can mirror or image its essence. The result is an activity or actualization (*energeia*) of the potential emanating from the essence; this manifested "offspring" constitutes the third axis. Thus emanation is revealed to be a cyclic relationship.

The Dyad is the number Two, but Rhea is a transcendent form of Two called the Indefinite Dyad (*hê Aoristos Duas*), where "indefinite" must be understood to mean indeterminate, unlimited, boundless, and infinite, all of which are relevant to the Indefinite Dyad. First I will focus on her property of being unlimited or indeterminate, which makes her the opposite of the Monad, who is the principle of limit, determination, and definition. Thus the Monad and Indefinite Dyad are the principles of limit (*peras*) and the unlimited (*to apeiron*), respectively, which operate at all levels of being, but in a different way on each level.

One of the most common names for the Indefinite Dyad is Dynamis, which means Power and Potential. This is the aspect of the Indefinite

Dyad in which she is unlimited, unbounded, and infinite, for hers is the infinite potential to be. She is potentiality at all levels of being, for she dares the Monad to proceed outward and to become. The Dyad is called the Goal, because she is that to which the Monad proceeds, and she is also called Daring and Change, for she brings the Monad into manifestation. She is more powerful than the Monad because, while the Monad is the power to be some specific thing, she is the limitless power to be any thing at all; she is all possibilities. Therefore the Indefinite Dyad is also the prolific, generative source of all creation. She is multiplying, for without her the Monad would be just One; she leads the Monad to proceed into fruitful plurality and substantial manifestation. Thus, on the lower levels of being she is called Life-Giving (*Zôogonos*).

Next I consider Kronos and Rhea in more detail.

Kronos

Aiôn is Eternity, that is, timeless time, the time outside of time. Time as we know it, determinate time, is created by the Monad and Indefinite Dyad, for Kronos is the abiding, but Rhea is the proceeding, who by her power to change entices the unchanging, self-limiting Kronos to proceed out from himself, and to become Khronos (Time) or Father Time. Moreover, as explained below, Rhea creates rhythm, and from the cyclic alternation of the opposites (light/dark, etc.), measurable time is born. Therefore, Plato (*Timaeus*, 37D) says that the Father creates Time as an animated image of Eternity (*Aiôn*). The word here translated "image" (*agalma*) refers especially to divine images set up in shrines and temples for veneration. We may see in this an allusion to the theurgic practice of "animating images," that is, of invoking a god into a statue, and thus our world is an ensouled, living image of Aiôn.

Creation of Zeus

The essence of Kronos is to remain, but Rhea has the power to cause him to proceed beyond himself. However, he must eventually revert or look back toward his essence to preserve his identity. In this way the determining, form-imparting power of the Monad emanates outward to inform matter, but it preserves its form by looking back toward its origin. For if this procession were to continue without limit or definition, all form would be lost in the dark abyss of indefinite chaotic matter.

Kronos' essence is to remain himself, but Rhea has the power to create another, and so from them Zeus is born. Thus the three phases — remaining, proceeding, reverting — create the Tridynamos, the threefold power of the triune godhead: Kronos, Rhea, Zeus. In the Chaldean Oracles we read:

The world, which saw thee, Threefold Monad, worshiped thee. (fr. 26)

This means the Threefold Monad contains the triad of Father, Mother, and Son. (The Chaldean Oracles are fragmentary poems dated to the second or third century CE, which Julian the Chaldean and his son, Julian the Theurgist, received by divine inspiration; Pythagoreans treat them almost as sacred scripture.)

The Platonic Ideas (Forms) exist in unity in the mind of Kronos, for he is the Monad, but Rhea has the power to discriminate the Ideas, for she is the Indefinite Dyad. Therefore in the mind of their son Zeus the Ideas are distinctly articulated, and become the Logos by which he creates the world. The Platonic Ideas have their origin in Kronos, the Father; they multiply without bound by the power of Rhea, the Mother; and they become active in the mind of Zeus, the Son. This is the esoteric meaning of the myth that Kronos swallowed his children — his Ideas — but that Rhea saved Zeus, who caused Kronos to vomit out the gods; thanks to Rhea and Zeus the gods are distinct beings. In summary, the gods of the Tridynamos govern three levels of reality: Being (*On*), Life (*Zôê*), and Mind (*Nous*). Referring to the Monad, the Chaldean Oracles say,

For with him is the Power, but from him is the Nous. (fr. 4)

As explained later, "Power" is another name for the Indefinite Dyad; thus the oracle says that Rhea is with Kronos, but Zeus is from him.

The Self-Contemplating Nous

This is an appropriate place to explain the concept of *noêsis* (intuitive thought), for both Kronos and Zeus have the character of an intuiting mind (*nous*). Although *noêsis* is sometimes translated "intellection," it does not refer to a process of discursive reasoning; rather, *noêsis* is a direct, intuitive apprehension of the essence of things. In contrast to reasoning, which occurs sequentially in time and deals with particulars located in space, *noêsis* is not bound by space or time (which occurs only at the level of the World Soul and below, for reasoning is an activity of the soul). Nous is timeless in essence, power, and activity; soul (*psychê*), however, is timeless in essence (for she is eternal), but temporal in activity, for her power brings the archetypal ideas into time.

The gods have *nous*, as do daimons, humans, and animals, for it is the divine part of their souls. That is, as there is a Cosmic Nous, so also each of our individual souls has a *nous*, the immortal divine part within, which understands meaning through a direct grasp of the eternal Ideas. (Pythagoras is credited with the discovery of the individual *nous*.)

The Nous has direct knowledge of the eternal Platonic Forms or Ideas, because it is of the same nature as them, but it cannot know the transient, changing individuals participating in those Forms, or anything that is formless. That is, we might say that the Nous is the archetypal mind (in Jung's terms, the collective unconscious), which has direct knowledge of the archetypes. (Therefore also, the gods, who reside in the Noetic Realm, cannot respond to us as individuals, but employ daimons as intermediaries.)

Both Kronos the Monad and Zeus the Demiurge can be characterized as cosmic minds (*noes*), but of different kinds. Kronos is a self-contemplating *nous*, that is, an inwardly directed mind, eternally at rest, for which the thinker and the thought are identical. He is utterly simple, because he transcends Form, of which he is the fount or source, and undivided. His is the level of pure being, and therefore he is the only one who has pure being as his sole object of thought. Thus Plato (*Cratylus*, 396b) suggests that Kronos' name means Pure Mind (*Koros Nous*, where *koros* signifies purity, *katharos*). He is called the Unmixed Nous, the First or Primal Nous, and the Paternal Nous. The Craftsman Zeus, in contrast, is an outwardly directed *nous*, who contemplates the Monad, articulating the Ideas in it by the separating power of the Indefinite Dyad. He is called the Demiurgic Nous, the Second Nous, and Nous Proper, for his active *noêsis* is most akin to our own. The Demiurge is often mistaken for the Father, for his work is more visible; as the Oracles say,

The Father finished every thing and handed them to Second Nous, whom you, the human tribe, call First. (fr. 7)

Here "finished" means "perfected," for Father Kronos thinks the model perfectly, but the Demiurge Zeus brings them into manifestation.

Kronos, as the Primal Nous, thinks the Ideas, but they exist in an undifferentiated unity, for he is the Monad. Therefore these unified Ideas are called *kurioi* (proper, supreme). The lords (*kurioi*), that is, the gods (the henads), also lie hidden at this level, and may be compared to the archetypes, which lie hidden in the unconscious until they choose to manifest in consciousness.

Rhea, the Indefinite Dyad, has the power to differentiate the Platonic Ideas and cause them to proceed outward from the source. Therefore her son Zeus thinks the articulated Ideas, that is, the Logos. The Monadic totality, the Idea of Ideas (*Eidos Eidôn*), provides the *Paradeigma* (Paradigm, Model) of the universe, which the Demiurge contemplates in his articulation of the Ideas and his creation of the world according to the Logos.

Zeus the Demiurge is called a Dyad, but this must not be confused with the Indefinite Dyad, his mother Rhea. (We might call him the Definite Dyad.) He is called a Dyad for two reasons. The first is because he is the son of Kronos the Monad; they are called the First and Second God, the First and Second Nous, the First and Second Fire, the Once and Twice (First and Second) Transcendent, and so forth. The second reason he is called Dyad is that he is a mediator between the empyrean (noetic) and material worlds. On the one hand, he contemplates the Ideas; on the other, he hurls his formative lightning bolts into the wombs of nature. This interpretation is confirmed by the Chaldean Oracles, which say of the Monad:

... beside this one a Dyad sits.
For he hath both: to hold noetics in his nous,
to bring sensation to the worlds.... (fr. 8)

That is, the Dyad Zeus, who sits beside the Monad Kronos, brings perceptible existence to the world by implanting the Forms in matter.

Kronos' realm is the primary cosmic order (*prôtos diakosmos*), the level of essential or real being (*to ontôs on*), and therefore of ultimate truth. However, because Kronos is identical to the absolute unity of his Ideas, the Chaldean Oracles tell us,

... the Father snatched himself away,
and didn't close his Fire in Noeric Power. (fr. 3)

That is, the supreme (*kurioi*) Ideas cannot be known by our unaided minds, for even our *nous* can comprehend the Ideas only as distinct and separate essences. Therefore the transcendent Monad is called indescribable, unnamable, ineffable, invisible, hidden, and the Paternal Abyss, for at the levels of Being (Kronos) and Life (Rhea) all possibilities occur simultaneously. However, by means of illumination (*ellampsis*) from the gods, *who see and know Abyss, Paternal, Hypercosmic,* (C.O. fr. 18) we may apprehend the Monad by means of our divine indwelling spirit, called "the Flower of the Nous." Kronos is the supreme simplicity of the First Mind as Rhea is the supreme simplicity of Primordial Matter (the universal foundation of all existence). Therefore they are both called Bythos (Abyss) and Bathos (Depth), for they are both impenetrably deep and profound. Proclus (c.411–485), Syrianus' successor, calls them "dissimilarly alike."

Primal Fire

Ancient Pythagorean doctrine (coming perhaps from Zoroaster) associates the Monad with the qualities light (as opposed to dark), hot, dry, light (vs. heavy), swift, and male, and associates the Indefinite Dyad with the opposite qualities. Since fire is hot and dry, the Monad and his offspring are especially associated with fire and the Sun. Similarly, the Zoroastrians say that the Father exists in beginningless light as the Mother dwells in endless darkness. Therefore we will see that the Sun is the preeminent symbol of the central male deities of Pythagorean theology.

First, Kronos is the Lord of Time (*Khronos*) and rules the Sun, who defines time by the alternation of night and day, and who governs nature through the cycle of the seasons. Therefore, the Chaldean Oracles call the First God the Transcendent Fire, and according to the emperor Julian (331–363 CE), this first principle is the Titan Hyperiôn (= He Above All), whom he identifies with Kronos, and who is the father of Helios.

The rays of the Primal Fire emanate throughout the universe, down through its levels, connecting it into one whole and harmonizing its parts. As the Oracles say,

All yield to the noeric lightning-storm of the
Noeric Fire and serve the Father's cogent will.
(fr. 81)

The lightning-storm (*prêstêr*) represents the illuminating Platonic Ideas, the rays that integrate and coordinate the universe. The Pythagoreans describe the seirai, the multilevel chords or chains that emanate from the Monad and tie the levels of reality together, allowing theurgists to ascend to Unity. The most important of these is the solar series (*Hêliou seira*), the central Axis of Light, which comprises the Monad (Kronos), the Demiurge (Zeus), the Transmundane Sun (Apollo), and the Mundane Sun (Helios). Each level has a Sun at its center, which unifies and governs that level and illuminates the lower levels. Also, each level is further removed from the original source of light (the Light of Lights) and more admixed with the dark; therefore each level partakes less of unity and more of diversity, and so there is a hierarchy of illumination. However, it is a mistake to think that the higher levels are better than the lower, for the light and the dark are necessary complementary poles of the All. From the One to prime Matter, the universe is an living image of divinity.

By means of the separating Power of the Indefinite Dyad, the Demiurge articulates the Platonic Ideas, creating the Logos and beginning the process of multiplication and generation by which the cosmos is born from the World Soul. Like a prism, which separates the colors from white light by bending the rays of each color in a direction unique to that color, but different from the other colors, so the Demiurge separates the Ideas by projecting them in accord with their essences. (This is, according to Empedocles, the power of Strife, which differentiates things by associating each with its own kind and separating it from other kinds; Strife is the divisive power of the Indefinite Dyad. Love, in contrast, draws all things together, regardless of kind; it is the unifying power of the Monad.)

Rhea

As explained above, the Indefinite Dyad, by bringing multiplicity to the One, creates the plurality of unities (henads), who are the gods. Thus Rhea becomes the Mother of the gods by substantiating multiple images of the Father, Kronos. Since Zeus is "father of gods and mortals," she is also called Amma (Grandmother).

Ever-Flowing Matter

At the most fundamental level, the Monad is primordial Form and the Indefinite Dyad is primordial Matter, the *prima materia* that is the indeterminate, formless, quality-less foundation of all being; she is sub-stance — she who stands underneath everything. Like the Monad, primordial Matter is ineffable, obscure, dark; therefore they are both called Abyss. Thus, the goddess of Matter is also called Silence (*Sigê*), because Silence must precede the Word, the in-forming Logos, embodying the Ideas of the Craftsman, Zeus. Her role as mediator between the father of the gods and the Demiurge is confirmed by the Chaldean Oracles:

between the Fathers is Hekáte's center borne.
(fr. 50)

(Proclus says that Hekate in Orphic theology corresponds with Rhea in Hellenic theology, who is between the First and Second Fathers.) Primordial matter is much deeper, more profound, than the matter studied by contemporary physics. Hers is potential corporeality, not a "stuff," but the unlimited power to become.

The ancient Pythagoreans called Rhea "the Ever-Flowing" (*to Aenaon*) and connected her name with *rheô* (to flow) and *rhoê* (flux, flow, stream), a derivation confirmed by modern linguistics, which traces them all to the Indo-European root *sreu-* (to flow). This is because primary matter is fluid, for it has no determinate boundaries, within or without; material existence is ever changing, always in flux.

Rhythm and Number

Another word correctly derived by the ancients from this root is *rhythmos*, which means rhythm, but also recurring motion, measured motion, and time. This is because the Indefinite Dyad creates otherness, and therefore all the polarities governed by Kronos and Rhea: unity/multiplicity, light/dark, male/female, and many others. Whenever there is a tension between opposites there will arise an oscillation between them, a cyclic approach to one and then a return to the other: the swing of the pendulum. Therefore, Rhea entices Kronos out of himself and transforms measureless Eternity (Aiôn) into determinate Time

(Khronos), symbolized by the cyclic alternation of light and dark. (By creating time, she also creates space.) Further, Rhea governs all cyclic processes, on earth and in heaven; she creates the universe as a *harmonia* of opposites. (See Opsopaus, "Lib. Oct. Mut." for universal structures in the tension of opposites.)

However, Rhea herself exists outside of time, and thus she governs motionless motion. This is because she is concerned only with cyclic change, and therefore with the numerical ratios among the rhythms of these changes; she governs their harmonic relations. She is Rhythmos (rhythm) as opposed to Khronos (time). (In modern scientific terminology, we could say that she oversees the "frequency domain" rather than the "time domain," which is the province of Hera, her daughter.)

The ancients also connected *rhythmos* to *arithmos* (number), but modern linguists trace *arithmos* to a different Indo-European root, *rê(i)-* (to reason, count), from which we also get such words as reason, rational, ratio, rate, and rhyme. Nevertheless, the ancient connection informs us about how Pythagoreans understand Rhea's responsibility for number. This is natural, for the Indefinite Dyad is the principle of plurality itself, which separates one thing from another, but also of the Matter that allows one thing to be different from another, by substantiating multiple instances of a Form or Idea.

Rhea governs the levels of being above the Logos or Intellect (Nous) of Zeus, which explains why a total grasp of number is beyond our intellectual abilities. (Modern mathematics addresses only an impoverished shadow of number.) The properties of number fall into two classes, corresponding to the last two phases of emanation: procession and reversion, for number combines the power to generate everything together with the power to unify everything. In particular, number discriminates the holistic thought of Kronos into the distinct Ideas, the articulate Logos, of Zeus. But also, by reversion, number redirects and reunifies the Ideas toward the Monad.

Living Matter

Recall that *noêsis*, which is usually translated intellection, is better understood as a process of holistic intuition, especially at this level, which is prior to time, and therefore prior to sequential thought. Rhea, as mediator, is the intellective (or noetic) process connecting the divine Intellect (Zeus) at the next lower level, with the object of his intellection, pure being (the Monad), at the next higher. But Rhea's domain is also the level of life, and therefore Proclus says, "Life is intellection" (*zôê noêsis*). On the one hand, this means that life is fundamentally identical to holistic intuition. On the other, it means that the Ideas are themselves living archetypes (not static concepts). The Chaldean Oracles tell us,

Of blessed Noerics Rhea is the source and stream;
for, first in Power, in wombs ineffable all things
receiving, on the All she pours this whirling brood.
(fr. 56)

The Noerics are archetypes living in the intuiting divine Mind, and may be identified with the gods. Rhea produces them from her divine womb, having separated them from union in the Monadic Nous (Kronos).

The etymological connection between "mother" and "matter" is well-known, but it is worthwhile to recall it. The Indo-European root *mâter* (mother) is the origin of our word "mother" and of the cognate Greek and Latin words (*mêtêr, mater*). The latter is the source of *matrix*, which originally meant a mother of any species, and by extension the womb or anything else in which something originates, develops, is nourished, or is contained. Matrix, in turn, is the root of "matter" and "material," which referred originally to an originating, nourishing, or sustaining substance. We have seen that the Mother is the life-giving goddess, the source of ever-flowing matter. Therefore she provides the quantities (measured by number) of matter needed for the sustenance of everything in creation. She is the ultimate cause of the primordial, life-giving, all-sustaining Earth.

Hesiod says that Helios is the son of the Titans Theia and Hyperiôn, but the emperor Julian identified Hyperion with Kronos. "Theia" of course means "divine female," but it is also a word for aunt and nurse; it is synonymous with "Têthis," which is connected with Têthys (Titan goddess of the Abyssal flux, nurse of Hera), another name for Hyperiôn's bride. Both names are related to Têthê (Allmother) and derived from a root meaning "to milk or suckle." In the Orphic theogony of Alcman (fl. 670 BCE), Thetis is the female aspect of the bisexual primordial Unity who governs Matter (*hulê*). Obviously these are all manifestations of the Great Mother Rhea, who gives substance to the world. As Hyperion and Theia, the Father and Mother engender a triad: the Sun (Helios), the Moon (Selene), and the Dawn (Eôs), who comes between the other two and signifies their union.

The Father and the Mother, having become two, now must dance to Rhea's rhythm. And this dance will bring them together again, for the Father has lust (*orexis*) for the Mother's body, and she desires to reproduce his Form. Through their conjunction, the Monad is divided by the Dyad, and Matter is unified by the One. From them come the creator and creatrix of the material world; thus the first generation, Kronos and Rhea, yields to the second, Zeus and Hera. Indeed, after the wedding, according to Pherecydes, Hera becomes Gaia, the goddess of the Earth as we know it.

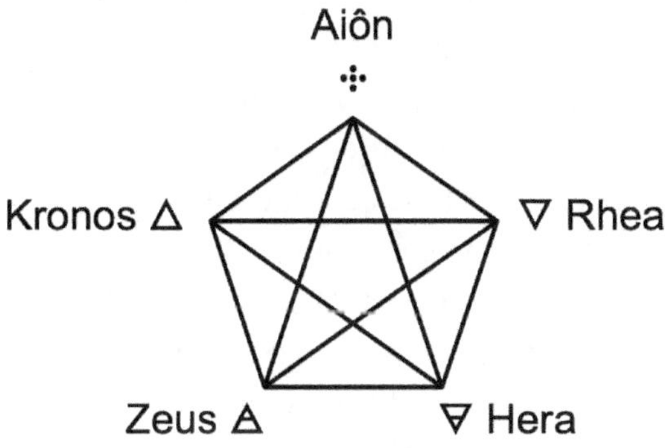

Creation of Hera

Zeus is the first of the Olympian generation born of the Titanic regents, Kronos and Rhea; the second is Hera, his sister and wife. She is the World Soul, who embodies in matter the articulated Ideas of Zeus. Pythagoreans differ about Hera's birth, but we may say that gods give birth by creating images of themselves, by a process of continuous emanation. Pherecydes implies that when Kronos and Rhea united, they transformed into Zeus and Gaia (here equivalent to Hera). Proclus, however, says that Zeus the creator makes the World Soul (Hera). In this case she may be seen as an image of Zeus in terms of rank and of Rhea in terms of character.

In any case, we have two ranks, Titanic and Olympian, with a god and goddess in charge of each. The emperor Julian (*Caesars*, 307CD) had a vision in which he saw them seated upon thrones: Kronos' was of black ebony of "a luster so intense and divine that no one could endure to gaze thereon"; indeed its intensity was greater than the Sun; this is the blinding blackness of the Paternal Abyss. Zeus's throne was of brilliant electrum, a union of gold and silver. (Êlektron, which may refer to amber as well as to the gold-silver alloy, is from the same root as Êlektôr, which is a name for the Sun.) On golden thrones were Rhea opposite Kronos, and Hera opposite Zeus.

In the material world these gods may be symbolized by the elements. Above them all is Aiôn, symbolized by the quintessence, which transcends the other elements. Fiery Kronos and fluid Rhea are opposites, descended from Aiôn, as symbolized by the opposed elements fire and water. Below them are the intellectual storm god Zeus and life-nurturing Hera (Gaia, according to Pherecydes), symbolized by the opposed elements air and earth. These relationships are neatly revealed by the pentagram, an ancient Pythagorean symbol (see figure). This diagram shows that Zeus and Hera each are born of both Kronos and Rhea, but that all four ultimately arise from Aiôn.

Creation of the Other Gods

Kronos and Rhea give birth to the other gods by a multiplication of unity. That is, the Mother, the Indefinite Dyad, as the principle of multiplicity, creates a plurality of images of the Monad, the Father. She causes separation and unlimited proliferation, but he maintains their definition by imposing limit on their identities. The result is a plurality of unities, which are called divine henads (units) and correspond to the gods. In the mind of Kronos they are individual yet interpenetrating, like the spectrum of colors in white light. As Proclus says, "All the henads are in all, but each separately." In Zeus's noetic realm, however, they become articulated as distinct divinities.

According to Proclus, some of the gods acquire their character from the triune nature of Ineffable Unity. The three phases of remaining, proceeding, and reverting correspond to three aspects of Unity: *peras* (limit), *to apeiron* (the unlimited), and *pronoia* (foreknowledge, providence); they reveal the essence, power, and activity of divinity, respectively. Each has a corresponding class of gods, who manifest its character.

Limit leads to father gods, who manifest limit, delimitation, definition, form, and law. At the noetic level (that of Zeus the Demiurge) and below they are often creators of some sort, for they create by imparting form to pre-existing matter. Notable among these is the Solar Series (described above).

The Unlimited leads to mother goddesses, who manifest the unlimited, indefinite, infinite, multiplying, productive, and generative powers. At the noetic level and below they are called life-giving.

Pronoia leads to the perfecting (*teleiôtikoi, telesiourgoi*) gods, who manifest foreknowledge and providence by assisting with the reintegration of the soul and its elevation to the gods. At the noetic level and below, some of these are called guardians (*phrourêtikoi*), because at these lower levels it is necessary to protect the essence of beings by preserving the distinctness of their forms. Others are called purifiers (*kathartikoi*) or liberators because they liberate and elevate the divine part of the soul.

The Names of the Gods

Isopsephy is the ancient art of exploring the esoteric meanings of Greek words by means of the numerical values of the Greek letters (similar to Hebrew gematria). For example, the Greek word for Monad, ΜΟΝΑΣ = 361, which may be reduced 3+6+1 = 10 and 1+0 = 1; therefore it reduces to 1, which is appropriate for the Monad. Similarly, the word for Dyad, ΔΥΑΣ = 605, which reduces to 2, also appropriate. Moreover, ΑΙΩΝ = 811, and therefore Aiôn reduces to 1, which is appropriate for the Ineffable Unity. The Titanic regents, Kronos and Rhea are the first two images of Aiôn. Now, ΚΡΟΝΟΣ does not reduce to 1, but Plato (*Crat.*, 396b) taught us that "Kronos" signifies *Koros Nous* (Pure Mind), and ΚΟΡΟΣ ΝΟΥΣ = 1180, which does reduce to 1 and suggests this is his true name. Iamblichus (c.245–c.325) tells us that the Dyad is called "Rhea," but PHA = 109, which reduces to 1, which is not correct for the Dyad, and so we may seek another name that better reflects her nature. Two of her standard epithets are Mother of Zeus (ΔΙΟΣ ΜΗΤΗΡ = 740) and Savior (Η ΣΩΤΕΙΡΑ = 1424); she is also called The Unlimited (ΤΟ ΑΠΕΙΡΟΝ = 686). All these reduce to 2 and symbolize her fundamental nature.

Bibliography

Much of this chapter is extracted from Opsopaus, "A Summary of Pythagorean Theology" (see below), where much more information can be found.

1. Athanassiadi, Polymnia. "A Contribution to Mithraic Theology: The Emperor Julian's Hymn to King Helios," *Journal of Theological Studies,* N.S., 28, Pt. 2, October 1977, 360–71. Helios as a mediating god; Hyperion identical to Kronos.

2. Burkert, Walter. *Lore and Science in Ancient Pythagoreanism,* transl. Edwin L. Minar, Jr. Cambridge: Harvard University Press, 1972.

3. Dillon, John, *The Middle Platonists: 80 B.C. to A.D. 220*, rev. ed. Ithaca: Cornell University Press, 1996.

4. Gwyn Griffiths, J. *Triads and Trinity.* Cardiff: University of Wales Press, 1996. A wide-ranging study of triads and triunities in the ancient world.

5. Iamblichus. *Theology of Arithmetic*, transl. Robin Waterfield. Grand Rapids: Phanes, 1988.

6. Kingsley, Peter. *Ancient Philosophy, Mystery, and Magic: Empedocles and Pythagorean Tradition.* Oxford: Oxford University Press, 1995. A comprehensive, profound study of the roots of the Pythagorean Tradition.

7. Lamberton, Robert. *Homer the Theologian: Neoplatonist Allegorical Reading and the Growth of*

the Epic Tradition. Berkeley: University of California Press, 1986.

8. Lewy, Hans. *Chaldean Oracles and Theurgy: Mysticism, Magic and Platonism in the Late Roman Empire*, new ed. by Michel Tardieu. Paris: Études Augustiniennes, 1978.

9. Majercik, Ruth. *The Chaldean Oracles: Text, Translation, and Commentary*. Leiden: E. J. Brill, 1989.

10. Opsopaus, John. "A Summary of Pythagorean Theology." 2002–4. omphalos.org/BA/ETP.

11. Opsopaus, John. "The Ancient Greek Esoteric Doctrine of the Elements." *Circle Magazine*, issues 68–71 (1998–9). Expanded version available at omphalos.org/BA/AGEDE.

12. Opsopaus, John. "Liber de Octo Mutationibus: The Book of Eight Changes: Universal Cycles and the Trigrams." 1995. omphalos.org/BA/LOM.html.

13. Opsopaus, John. "Orphica Holodemiurgia." 1998. Available at omphalos.org/BA. The annotated version contains additional information on Aiôn, Time, the Celestial Spheres, etc.

14. Plato. *Plato's Cosmology: The Timaeus of Plato*, translated with a running commentary, by F. M. Cornford. New York: Humanities Press, n.d., c.1937.

15. Plutarch. "Isis and Osiris," in *Moralia*, vol. V, transl. F. C. Babbitt. Loeb Classical Library, Cambridge: Harvard University Press, 1936.

16. Proclus. *On Plato Cratylus,* intro., transl., & notes, Brian Duvick. London: Bloomsbury, 2014.

17. Proclus. *The Elements of Theology*, 2nd ed., rev. text, transl., & comm., E. R. Dodds. Oxford: Oxford University Press, 1963.

18. Proclus. *The Theology of Plato*, transl. Thomas Taylor. Vol. VIII of Thomas Taylor Series. Somerset: Prometheus Trust, 1995.

19. Sallustius. *Concerning the Gods and the Universe*, ed. with proleg. & transl., A. D. Nock. Chicago: Ares Publishers, 1996; reprint of Cambridge, 1926, ed.

20. Schibli, Hermann S. *Pherekydes of Syros.* Oxford: Oxford University Press, 1990.

21. Siorvanes, Lucas. *Proclus: Neo-Platonic Philosophy and Science.* Edinburgh: Edinburgh University Press, 1996.

22. Watkins, Calvert (ed.). *The American Heritage Dictionary of Indo-European Roots*, 2nd ed. Boston: Houghton Mifflin Company, 2000. Modern etymology.

23. West, M. L. *Early Greek Philosophy and the Orient*. Oxford: Oxford University Press, 1971. Zurvân, Zoroastrianism, etc.

Meditation With the Earth Mother Goddess, Cybele

by Rev. Donna M. Swindells

Imagine you are a traveler to a foreign land. You hope to find the Great Mother Goddess Cybele's temple. You desire to see her in her glory. As you approach her temple, the wind carries the smell of pine trees that surround her sanctuary. You now see Her Temple. Words fail to express its beauty. Huge pillars support its lofty roof. It is bright because of the hundreds of candles burning in devotion & petition to her.

You hear the roar of lions, as Cybele's golden chariot pulls up at the entrance. Then you see with your eyes the Goddess herself. Great indeed is she! Upon her head sits a crown, with a sheer veil of glittering stars attached. Even under her veil, you see her long, black hair. Her face is beautiful to behold. Her eyes are large & expressive. They twinkle like diamonds as she looks at the crowd. Cybele's lips are red, like a pomegranate. Her cheeks are rosy. Dressed in midnight blue, her dress shines with gems & pearls.

You feel yourself being pulled by her strong presence. Cybele locks eyes with you. She smiles at you. You are invited to enter with her into the temple. The sweet smell of incense hits your senses. You already feel the magic & electricity in the air.

As you follow behind the Goddess Cybele, she is handed a frame drum. Cybele shakes it, and then leads the beat. Men & Women join in the rhythm of the Goddess. Some dancers are wearing animal skins. Some wear sheer silk, shimmering on their bare skin. The sound of the flutes, lyres and castanets join in the ever- growing sound.

Red & white rose petals fall upon Cybele & you. You now are the only one following her to her throne. Cybele approaches her throne & stands. You kneel at the Goddess' feet. She takes your face into her hands. She is communicating to you through your mind. Her words pierce your heart. Her powerful presence fills your body. She pulls back her hands, releasing you from the secret communication that only you have heard.

Cybele motions to one of her priestesses. She brings a small bottle of sweetest oil to her. The Goddess anoints your forehead. This oil opens up your third eye. You now see the pure holiness of this Mother Goddess. She is the Mother of Gods & Goddesses. Her presence gives cities protection, just by having her statue venerated. In this sacred temple, you see the black meteorite that fell from the heavens. This is the holy stone of Cybele. It stands beside her throne. Cybele asks you to kiss this stone of hers. You place your lips upon it. It feels cool to them. In an instant, you are transported by Cybele. You are traveling in a golden chariot by her side. She has taken you on a journey across the night sky.

She lands the chariot & shows you former places of where she was worshipped long ago. Cybele points out mountain tops & caves. She shows you the cave where Zeus was hidden from view & raised. Also, she talks to you about the God Dionysus. Cybele talks about how the madness affected him. He was weak & tired when he reached her temple. She tells you she used her magical arts & healing powers to remove Hera's curse upon him. Cybele shows you how the sacred places where the Gods & Goddesses are now replaced by other religions. Also, she lets you see some temples that still lay buried. You see the sadness in her eyes, of days past. It is possible for a Goddess to weep. You feel the weight of her heart.

She tells you it is time to return. Cybele leads you to her lions. You slowly stroke their manes. These mighty lions purr with a low sound. What an honor to be allowed to touch them! You climb aboard her golden chariot. Cybele takes you back to her temple. You see a shooting star as you descend from the sky. As you land, she kisses you on your lips. Pure electric current runs through your body. Now you see Cybele in her full glory. Cybele is the Mistress of animals. Many animals circle her, as she is fully revealed. In Her splendor, Cybele is not wearing a queenly crown. Or dressed in a midnight blue gown. No gems or pearls. Cybele in

Her glory wears a crown of violets. Her clothes are the many-colored leaves of the forest. She shines with the colors of the rainbow itself. The Goddess Cybele slowly fades away from your sight. You hear her whisper, "I will see you again, in your dreams." As you come back to yourself, you are back in your home. Take your time to sit up & clear your head.

As you come back to yourself, eat & drink something. This will help you avoid a headache, due to your meditation. When encountering a Divine God or Goddess in a deep meditation, you need some time also to come back to yourself.

I hope your encounter with Cybele was amazing, full of wonders. Write down anything that you experienced during your encounter. This is an outline for a meditation. Your experiences may & will vary. Let yourself go at any point of this meditation. Ask Cybele to guide your spiritual encounter.

Praise to the Magna Mater Cybele

by Rev. Donna M. Swindells

Upon Mt. Ida's lofty heights,
Dwells a Goddess of ecstatic rites.
The sound of clashing cymbals & shields ring out,
As Her faithful celebrate & loudly shout.
The beating of drums echo throughout the night.

Head tossed back & eyes alive with fire
Your love the Gods themselves desired
Lovers of yours come and go
One you loved was your story of woe
Attis' life by his own hand expired.

Healer of Dionysus, Zeus' beloved son
From madness the curse by you undone.
He your student learned your mysteries
By your instruction changing our history
Dionysus for us our freedom won.

Magna Mater of the fragrant pines,
Your beauty is sublime
Playing the frame drum, dancing so free,
Your devoted children filled with glee,
Filled with Dionysus' sweet red wine.

Lady of Lions, defender of towns.
You adorn yourself in Nature's gown.

Leaves of black & violet flowers crowned.
For generations your story is told.
May your praises loudly resound.

❖ 76 ❖

Prayer to the Great Mother Rhea-Kybele

by Robin Wilcox

We pray to the Supreme Mother for Her blessing. Mother, may we have from You the blessings of health, wisdom, patience, courage, and safety.

Mother, come forth from Your mountain home and sit beside us all. Allow us to take shelter at Your immovable feet.

August Goddess, we ask that You protect us from tyranny, and from all who wish us harm.

May all that happens be Your will, O Queen of Queens.

May our will reflect Yours, as Your will is only Good.

<u>Rhea the Mother</u>

by Rachel Iriswings

Hail to Rhea, Fertile Woman,
Matriarch of the Theoi!

The waters of life are Yours, and they flow freely
You provide comfort and ease
Your guidance brought Zeus to His throne

To celebrate our mothers and maternal figures
is to celebrate within Your domain
When we honor them, we honor You

I ask You to watch over those
who have the courage to sacrifice,
to give of themselves for the children
Through them, time flows
Through them, ancestry rises
Please protect and support them, Mother Rhea!

Rightly I Am Called

by Rebecca Buchanan

She came over the mountains
        over the hills
        over the plains
        through forests and valleys
Her long hair dragging behind
        entangling trees
        rocks
        lions
        wolves
Banging her drums
Shaking her bracelets
        her anklets
King of the Gods, he calls himself
        claiming throne and sky
        — he even tried to steal my drums,
        hurling thunder
But Mother of All the Gods am I
My daughters and sons are sky
        and sea and
        earth and underearth
Spirits of flame
        and salt water and
        wood and cave
Rightly I am called
Great Queen
Good Goddess
Mother of Mountains

As I dance and
     sing and
     drum
Across the world

*[Author's Note: after an anonymous inscription
found at Epidauros]*

The Titans: Twelve Hourglasses

by Rebecca Buchanan

Theia
I am the eldest child
of heaven and earth.
Far-shining
one,
bright-shining,
one, I bestow gold
and glory on the daring.

Hyperion
I am the high one, ever
watchful, all-seeing,
the source of
all
wisdom. I am
the father of sun,
moon, and dawn, who share my gifts.

Tethys
I am the mother of all
waters. The rivers
and seas are
my
children. See
the diving bird and
know that I fathom your grief.

Okeanus
I am the ouroboros,
the great river that
encircles
the
world, the border
between living and
dead. Stars bathe in my waters.

Mnemosyne
I am memory, cosmic
and ancestral. Drink
my waters
to
remember,
Lethe's to forget.
The consequences are yours.

Krios
I am the curly-hornéd
ram, the navel star
whose rising
marks
the rebirth
of the year. The winds
and the stars are my children.

Themis
I am natural law, the
custom of ages.
I wield the
scales
of justice,
but I am not blind,
ever fair, never wrathful.

Iapetus
I am the piercer, the spear
of mortality
who offers
fame
in death. My
sons are arrogant,
rash, violent, and crafty.

Phoebe
I am the foreseeing one,
the first oracle.
At Delphi
I
sat enthroned,
a gift of earth, snakes
ever whispering secrets.

Koios
I am the celestial
axis, the constant
stellar pole
'round
which heaven
revolves, the ever
questioning rational mind.

Rhea
I am the ground upon which
the winds and the sea
depend. I
ride
my lions
to the song of drums
between city and mountain.

Kronos
I am the youngest, I who
wielded the scythe that
cut earth from
sky,
allowing
life to flourish. I
sleep in the caverns of night.

To Dione

by Ariadne Rainbird

Divine One, beautiful Dione
Daughter of Heaven and Earth
Who by Zeus, to Aphrodite Pandemos gave birth
Most lovely of nymphs, Fair One bright
Titaness Goddess, of oracular sight
Whose priestesses and prophetesses of
Hellas's most ancient shrine
At Dodona, where You shared with Zeus the
          oracle divine
Were called Peleiades or the Doves,
The sacred birds of the Goddess of love
For a black dove it is said to Dodona flew
And commanded that an oracle be built to You
And to Zeus, whose temple You shared
Equal in power and honour, revered
Zeus's ancient consort and Prometheus's bride
Who awakens the powers which within us reside
Yours is the healing vitality that radiates
From the centre of our selves, opening the
          subtle gates
The vital force Nourishing body and soul
Bringing spiritual prosperity, making us whole
O vision of beauty, linking below and above
Set of emotions, Mother of love,
Bring me healing, vitality, balance and power
May I prosper and blossom like an unfolding

flower
Stretch my soul, open my mind
To Divine Harmony, Oh Goddess kind

To Kronos

by Ariadne Rainbird

Father of Gods, from Whom the Mighty Ones
      Proceed
Supreme Kronos, The Elder Olympians Thy seed
Who permeates all, and absorbs all back into Thee
Restoring all, from whom all forms come to be,
Incorruptible, Noetic, Great Awakener, who propels
      the Mind
Lord of all progress, setter of measurable time
Pure Intellect Who rules the Golden Age
Progeny of Gaia and Ouranus, Prometheus-like
      Sage
Bearing a sickle you carve the zodiac into the sky
Allowing mankind to observe and measure the time
      passing by
Husband of Rhea, Who governs the flow of time
Mighty Bearer of the Rod, King Sublime
Presiding over the realms of Heroes Divine
The awakened mind, the enlightened soul, is Thine.
O Mighty Titan, Krouown ton Noun, Who strikes
      the mind
Awaken our minds and souls that we may find
The blissful state of the Golden Age within the soul
Grant a blessed, fruitful life, true and whole.

<u>To Rhea</u>

by Ariadne Rainbird

Blessed Rhea, Great Goddess profound
Kronos's Great Queen with turrets crowned
Mother of cities and the mountains wild
Protectress of the Divine Child
Rich-haired Mother of Gods and man
Illustrious Queen, Holy Titan
O Great Mother, Holy One come!
Ecstatically beating Your cymbal and drum
O Lady of the flow of time
Majestic Queen, holy and sublime
Liberating Goddess we honour Thee
Lady of abundance, wild and free,
Throned on a chariot by mighty lions drawn,
Of gentle Gaia and lofty Ouranus born
The vast mountains, the deeply spreading sea
And the aetherial gales proceed from Thee
Come Great Mother and hear our mystic pleas
Bring rich abundance, comfort and ease

To the Titans

by Ariadne Rainbird

O Blessed Gods to Thee I pray
Eos who heralds the light of day
Spreading with joy your rosy glow
Awaken my mind, my body and soul
O gracious Goddess of the dawn
Through Thee each new day is born
As rises high the Golden Sun —
Helios the all-seeing one
O Mighty Titan, Lord of light
Who rules the day with unconquered might
Watch over me Lord, I plea
And steer me on the path of piety
Theia Euryphaessa's Mighty Son
 — The Far Shining Goddess of inspiration
And who's Father is Hyperion
 — Lord of light, the All High One
O Titans, powers of natural law
Forefathers and mothers of natures awe
I call on Thee — expand my soul and mind
Great Iapetus, ancestor of mankind
Thou who governs mortality
May my life be true, just, and worthy
Thæmis, Divine Law, Justice and Truth
Of Oracular power, giver of sooth
Mother of the blessed Horai
And Who bore by Zeus, the holy Moirai

Eunomia, Dike, Eirine, never cease,
In giving Wise counsel, justice and peace
Clotho, Lachesis and Átropos, fates dread,
Spinner, measurer and cutter of life's thread
Prometheus too was sprung from Thee, Titans great
Who's name means Foresight, seeing our fate
Who brings progress and the holy fire
That illumines our minds and sparks our desire
To create and to grow to learn and problem solve
Who with Blessed Dioni helps us evolve
O Dioni, Oracle and prophetess,
Sister to Phoebe, Mnemosyne and Themis
Each Titan and Titaness with a unique role
In awakening and stretching the human soul
Okeanus, the river that around the earth flows
Firstborn Titan from whom Gods and men arose
Help us connect to the source of our being
The waters of life forever overseeing
The Okeanides are Thy blessed daughters
With Tethys, Mother of rivers, clouds and
         fresh waters
I give honour to Thee Gods of primal creation
Accept my offerings and adoration
Kreios who measures the temporal portions
         of the year
Let me tread the path with a heart with no fear
Thou who governs the stars, and beginnings anew
Let me face each beginning with a heart that is true
And Blessed Mnemosyne, Thee I beseech

To bless me with memory and the power of speech
For time destroys all, yet itself is immortal
Whilst memory preserves, and opens the portal
To a life that's divine, blessed and free
I call on the bright one, the Goddess Phoebe
In whom the sources of oracular ability we find
And Koios, Titan of the questioning mind
By Koios, Phoebe bore Astæría, the starry one,
          bright
Goddess of falling stars and oracles of night
Who, bore Hekate, the holy dark maiden,
Goddess of Virtue who reveals what is hidden
And Phoebe by Koios also Leto bore
Who bore the divine twins, on Delos's shore.
And I call on great Rhea, mother and queen
And Kronos who ruled the Golden age supreme
Who wears the crown and holds the rod
That passes the power from God to God
O blessed Titans I honour you all
And pray You hear Your mystic's call.

The Heavens
And the Deep

❖

Uranus and the Dance of the Stars
by Karl Friedrich Schinkel

<u>Helios</u>

by Rebecca Buchanan

Not yet, the rising of the Sun
Not yet, the radiance of my Lord —

birds i hear birds!
ecstatic song
is it time?
is it time?

The coming of the Sun
The coming of my Lord —

light i see light!
painful sweet
he is come!
he is come!

My Lord Helios is come!

[Author's Note: after Antal]

<u>Hymn to Helios I</u>
by Rebecca Buchanan

helios
solar-wreathed
king of day
whose light nourishes the earth:

i sing you glory

Hymn to Okeanos

by Rebecca Buchanan

Okeanos
Father of Salt Waters and Sweet
Who girdles the world:

The rivers and the seas are your children

<u>Hymn to Selene III</u>
by Rebecca Buchanan

bright curling ram's horns:
hair of deepest night:
gown of moonlight and shadow:
in the stillness
before the dawn
you embrace your lover
in his bed of sweet grass and soft flowers:
fifty daughters you have borne
womb swelling
and a lone sleepless son:
does he feel your kisses?

Leto's Gift

by Rebecca Buchanan

Sing Muses
Of that glorious day
When winsome-eyed Leto
Bore her greatest gift

Sing Muses
As the rocks sang
As Winds and Ocean sang
As the whole of Creation rejoiced

Sing Muses
Of the birth of golden-bright Apollon
And forest-dark Artemis
Beloved children of gentle-hearted Leto

[Author's Note: after Limenios]

<u>Ouranos</u>

by Rachel Iriswings

cloudwatching
aspiration
reach up
freedom in flight

fresh winds
clear breaths
endless heavens

stargazing
inspiration
stretch out
wisdom in height

abyssal depths
celestial wonders
all-embracing

<u>Ouranos on the Westbound 5:14</u>

by Tisdale Flannery

He rolls, slightly, with the movement of the cars, the gentlest of jostling, foray and return. The slump of his body against the greasy window is not the posture of defeat, but of patience; he has been here, on the molded plastic seat, for far too long, but his expression is alert and there is a sparkle in his eye.

"You know how they did it, don't you?" he asks, speaking only to you, as you face him across the aisle. "How they castrated me, I mean."

You wince, and glance around at the other passengers, but no one seems to have even heard him.

He continues, his voice clear and resonant. He is as oblivious to them as they are to him. "When I lay with her, when the battles and struggles and victories of the day were all done, and my desire raged; when I came to the Earth to spill myself upon her in triumph and the natural will to power. I came to her, and I covered her with darkness. This is when they ambushed me. This is when my sons pinned my four limbs, and with his sickle my clever son cut off my fifth." He says this without rancor. "They spilled me, alright — spilled my blood out upon the earth, and my seed in the water. Red ran the mud, and the foam crashed in the water, and great and beautiful things came from it."

You recoil from the dirt beneath his horn-like fingernails as he reaches out and points at you, his finger to your face. "Like you. Like you, human creature, great and beautiful and terrible, covering the earth with your achievements. Spilling out your civilization. Buildings. Cities. Roads. Covering the Earth in triumph of your own." He pulls his crabbed hand back to his chest. "You were the child of that violence."

He closes his eyes. Silvery whiskers stipple his lower cheeks and chin, and the long hairs in his eyebrow move questioningly, antennae on this human face. "Kronos ruled after me. A Titan, chosen by his own mother, courage in his hands and in his adamantine sickle. But the same sickness that chained me to my fate, also bound him to his; he feared his own creations, and hid them within himself. I buried mine; he ate his. It was the same. Likewise, his children after that, and after that. They live in fear of the setting sun." He bows his head and cups his hands. "We are all fools."

A woman in a burgundy suit passes by and drops a few shiny coins into his palms. He opens his eyes and stares for a moment. She is already moving through to the next car, maybe to escape his body odor. A smile twists from his mouth. "We never learn, do we? Always, we want to hold onto our rule. Always, we need to protect ourselves from what comes after." He shakes his shaggy head, and his long, dirt-colored hair brushes the squirrel-fur trim on his parka. "You have inherited this from us, I know. You, child of man, and children of the gods. You who rule the earth by virtue of your ability to destroy it. You hold on to what is yours, and cannot let go — you take, and keep. The oceans, the mountains, the oil beneath the rock — this you take, and burn, and use the fires to hold off what comes next."

He leans forward. He looks right in your face — Ouranos, father of the gods. His eyes are not the blue of the sky. His eyes are the sky, and his face is creased with ridges and canyons that came and went before you knew time. He whispers to you. His breath reeks of the tomb. "And I think you know what comes next."

Ouranos gets off on the next stop. You stay on the train, rolling with its movement. You are almost at the end of the line. The auto dealerships and chain hotels fill the landscape outside the subway window, covering the earth as far as the eye can see.

<u>A Prayer to Leto</u>

by Rachel Iriswings

Praise to the gentle Mother, modest Leto,
long-lived Titan; daughter of
Koios the Northern pillar of Heaven
and Phoebe: bright, pure, Prophetess;
sister of the Falling Stars,
Who blessed You with relief
when You endured endless pursuit and labor

May we always honor Your works
and celebrate Your presence as
moonlit Artemis and shining Apollon do!
Be at peace and smile upon us all!

<u>Prayer to Leto I</u>

by Rebecca Buchanan

Star-crowned Leto
Deepest Dark
Gentle enfolding night
Sweet nocturnal breeze:
Hold me in Your warm embrace

Selene
by Ariadne Rainbird

To Helios for Therino Iliostasio

by Ariadne Rainbird

[Author's Note: to be recited during summer solstice celebrations]

Glorious Golden Helios
As your fiery globe rises on this the longest day
Shed light on our deeds
That we may be guided by Your holy rays
May our lives be filled with blessedness
As Your golden rays caress the sacred Earth
O guardian of oaths, who surveys all
Bless us with Your healing rays
And may we strive to live with Arete
All-seeing Titan, life-giving Sun
With wisdom, strength and honour
May we be endowed
To courageously fight for what is right
Watched over by Your All-seeing eye

To Hyperion

by Ariadne Rainbird

O Titan God of Heavenly light
Giver of the gift of sight
Sire of Golden Helios and Selene bright
Whose rays light up the day and night
Hyperion we call to You

Titan Son of Earth and Sky
O You who watches from on high
Gazing upon all with wisdom's eye
Spouse to Theia of the clear blue sky
Hyperion we call to You

You order the bright bodies that adorn
The heavens with celestial form
Sun and Moon, and dusk and dawn
Which cause each day to be born
Hyperion we call to You

O Primal God of the Eastern skies
Where first does rosy Eos rise
Hailing Helios, of the All-Seeing eyes
O God of light and enlightenment, wise
Hyperion, we call to You

Giver of seasons, of night and day
May Your Divine light guide our way

Illumine our minds with the wisdom You purvey
Bless Your mystics on the path we pray
Hyperion, we call to You!

❖ 108 ❖

To Kreios

by Ariadne Rainbird

Father of stars, ram-horned, heart of the sky
Who's rising constellation marks time passing by
Strong leader, Hailer of the Spring,
Rising from the South as the agricultural
      year begins
Mighty Kreios, who orders the measures of the year
Joined in love with bright Eurybia
Astraeus, Persus And Pallas Thy mighty sons
Titan God of constellations, of stars and suns
Primordial God, brother to Hyperion bright
Lord of the stars that shine at night
O Giver of things of benefit to mankind
Who blesses fields and crops with benignant mind
Guardian of the southern sky, and sailor's guide
Over the turning seasons You preside
O Megamedes You of lasting fame
Stir our hearts and souls to noble aim
As Golden Helios enters your sign let light increase
And bless us with abundant harvest and
      healing peace

<u>To Leto</u>

by Ariadne Rainbird

Gentle Leto, modest and pure,
Kindest of Gods, with womanly demure
Progeny of Koios and Phoebe bright,
Sister to Asteria of the starry night
Titan Goddess of Motherhood,
Glad of Heart, Mild and good
Blessed Bride of Zeus, dark-gowned, obscure,
Restless wanderings were yours to endure
Driven on, by Python Pursued,
Til at blessed Delos your wanderings conclude
There, grasping wild olive and palm,
You gave birth, concealed from harm,
To the Divine twins, Apollon bright,
And Artemis fair, whom arrows delight.
Glorious Goddess, motherly queen
Issuing light from darkness, seen from unseen.
O Seemly Goddess, majestic and fair
Slim of waist, with lovely hair
To Gods and mortals always kind
Look upon me I pray with benevolent mind.
Goddess of the distaff, gold,
May your holy mysteries unfold.
Help me in times of adversity, to endure
O gracious Goddess, mild and pure.

<u>To Okeanus</u>

by Ariadne Rainbird

Eldest of the Titans, of Gaia and Great Ouranus
        spawned
Deep swirling Okeanus, serpentine and bull-horned,
Earth encircling power, life begetting Lord
Most Fertile of Gods, from whom 3,000 rivers
        poured,
Husband of Tethys, and origin of all,
Loud-booming Father of the Okeanides, I call
Whose primordial water around the heavens flows
Incorruptible source of bliss, from whence Gods
        and men arose
Your light-footed daughter's, scattered far, keep
In their care the earth and the waters deep
Girdled with the circle of the sky
Source of earth's waters, producing rain from high
You set the limits of the earth, surrounding all.
Come Blessed Titan, hear you supplicant's call.
May your purifying waters cleanse me body
        and soul
That with a pure heart I, aspire to a pure goal.

<u>To Selene</u>

by Ariadne Rainbird

Beautiful, benevolent, clear source of light
In the heavens shining, torch of the night
Daughter of Hyperion The High Lord of Light
and wide-shining Theia Euryphaessa bright
Sister to Golden Helios who's fire lights the day
Reflecting His glory with gentler ray
O All-Shining Pasiphae, You sweep through the
        night sky
In Your winged horse-drawn chariot, riding high
Bringer of peace, blessed foe of strife
Aid us Blessed Goddess to a blameless life
With Your shining veil diffusing silver rays
Divine Aigle, Your radiance lights our ways
Bringing light to the darkness, illuminating, clear
Cleansing and purifying, banishing fear
Queen of the stars, Goddess sublime
Wandering through the night, Measurer of time
O All-Seeing Mene, Just Goddess, we praise
Shine on our rites with beneficent rays

<u>Whither Atlas?</u>

by John Muro

Perhaps it was the want for solace or
Certainty that brought me back to see
What was left of the abandoned building
That was slowly being swallowed by
Dog-eared under-growth, green creepers
And tendrils of ornate calligraphy sprawled
Across the white walls of ripening decay.
The structure abutted a glum corridor of
Interstate where a penitent titan once
Kneeled atop the roofline and hoisted a
Ponderous earth, slowly spinning thru dull,
Dead air before he was sundered by a
Hammer-claw of wind or perhaps he had
Simply seen too much of this world and,
Disenchanted, boarded a ghost ship from
The harbor back to Olympus and the safe-
Keeping of his many daughters. Year's on,
A man mired in middle-age with little hope
In his heart, recalls the stern admonishments
Of the sisters who, decades before, declared
That he was, in fact, our every-man, bearing
With uncommon grace, and since before the
Time of angels, the darker burden of sin. Yet,
I remember thinking, with eyes half asleep
Behind my wooden desk, that he, too, would
Eventually leave us, tossing this round world

Like some counterfeit currency into the wilds
of wind.

❖

*Atlas and the Hesperides by John Singer Sargent.
Currently in the Museum of Fine Arts Collection,
Boston, MA, USA.*

Memory, Intellect, and Time

Prometheus Forms Man and Animates Him With the Fire From Heaven, from Ovid's Metamorphoses. The workshop of Hendrick Goltzius (1588-1590).

<u>Lethe</u>

by John Muro

Half-awake sleeping,
A lightness settles
Over eyes and limbs
Chest lifting,
As if in dream,

Like the line between
Despair and anguish.
Now I'm swimming
In pearl-gray water, metal-
Bright. I'm thinking,

I might yet go under.
Soon, I'm drifting,
And memory, from shore,
Unwhispers me asleep
And I cannot wake.

Hollowed bones ache,
And a keel-deep
Calm follows. Vapor-
Soft eyes can hear lightning
Without sound or wind or thunder.

<u>Mnemosyne</u>

by Suz Thackston

Bodiless and weightless, you float. There is no time. There is nothing until you realize that you are aware of the nothing. A single thought bobs about you, a toy boat on the surface of a dark ocean. The journey was so long. So long. You want to fall back into the nothing, but now you are dark and deep, not nothing any more.

You drag yourself up from the depths as though moving through thick water. The effort overwhelms you. For a time you stay still, silent, barely conscious.

Finally you open your eyes. You are surprised to find sunlight, a mild blue sky, gently moving tree branches above you. You push yourself up from where you were lying. You are next to an old stone wall enclosing a riot of trees. Nearby is a wooden gate, also old, shabby, but standing invitingly open.

You step into the garden, feet sinking into the springy turf. A broad path unfurls before you, studded with periwinkles. Sunlight pours like thin honey over the trees and tall shrubs. You can just see a smaller pathway branching off from the main one, coy, glimmering, obscured by clumps of daisies and curtains of moss.

It is so quiet. The leaves whisper, and there is a distant trickle of water, but no birdsong or insect hum intrudes.

You walk through the quiet sunlight, the dreaming trees. As you approach the branching pathway a violet butterfly detaches itself from a tulip and flits down the little path. You follow.

You see a white cypress leaning over a pool. The pool is small, still, dark. The delicate branches of the cypress and the placid sky overhead are reflected in its surface. A dragonfly hovers above it on shimmering rainbow wings. It lands on the water. You can see tiny dimples where its feet touch.

You take a step closer. The water is so still and pure. You realize that your throat is parched. You know how the water will feel sliding down your throat, cool and sweet. You move toward the pool.

A raven croaks from a thicket to your right. He flutters to the ground before you and cocks his head to one side, staring at you from a bright black eye. You regard each other for a long moment. Then you turn from him, back to the quiet pool.

The raven hops over to you, his thick beak angled at your bare toes. You shoo him. He retreats, but in a moment he moves in close again. He emits a harsh cry. He flies a short distance, perching near an obscure little path winding around a white-blossomed pear tree before it disappears into the foliage. He gronks again, flapping.

With a sigh you turn from the little pool and the silent cypress, your dry throat aching. The raven gives a satisfied 'tock', watching you from a low branch of the pear tree. The path, dim in the thick green, leads you to an opening between two rowans.

A clearing lies before you, filled with the small music of a spring. The water bubbles up around mossy rocks and runs away under a little stone bridge, disappearing into the depth of the garden.

You move toward it, thirsty, enchanted. But before you reach it there is a rustle in the underbrush. A snake, glimmering jewel tones spangled down its length, slides through the grass. It coils between you and the spring. Its black eye is like that of the raven, bright and blank.

There is a flash of gold on the far side of the spring. A lion leaps across the ribbon of clear water, small but rippling with muscle under the taut tawny hide. It steps carefully around the snake and lies down a few feet from you. You think its eyes will be bright golden, but they too are black.

The raven croaks softly behind you. You glance back at it, then before you at the spring, and the snake, and the lion. For a long time none of you move a muscle.

You open your mouth, perhaps to plead with them to let you through to the bright water, or maybe to shout and try to scare them away. But to your surprise what comes from you is a song. After the first thin notes it pours forth from your throat, and you wonder how you could have forgotten the song, the spell, the incantation.

> *I am a child of Earth and starry Heaven,*
> *But my race is of Heaven alone.*
> *This you know yourselves.*
> *I am parched with thirst and perish;*
> *But give me quickly refreshing water*
> *Flowing forth from the Lake of Memory.*

Your song dies away among the flowers. The snake lowers its head. It uncoils and slides smoothly to a boulder in the sun where it drapes itself indolently, watching you, but no longer blocking your access to the stream. The lion rises, stretches, yawns, and pads to the sparkling stream. It leaps back across and settles into a curled ball on the far side. Its jet eyes close.

You feel small pricks in your shoulder as a heavy weight lands on you. The raven's thick beak is right next to your eye. You stand motionless. The raven ruffles its feathers impatiently and grumbles. It jerks its beak toward the stream.

It stays on your shoulder, gripping with talons that almost pierce your skin, as you kneel before the stream and drink deeply. The water is shockingly cold, making your teeth ache, but it slips into your body like silk, like light. You feel a surge of energy.

You rise, the raven rising with you, and move deeper into the garden.

As you round a shrub heavy with redolent pink blossoms a round pit of darkness opens under your feet. You stagger and jerk back, but you are too late. The garden rushes up past you as you plummet into the black. The raven chuckles softly and lifts, leaving you to fall down the well by yourself.

Before the scream building in your throat can burst free you are in a familiar place. The fragrance of flowers fills your head, and you are four years old, playing hide and seek with your best friend. Laughter bubbles through you. You thrum with unbearable excitement as you shriek and run, looking behind the trees and hedges of this wonderfully familiar back yard.

You round a corner and the world shifts. Pain floods you. You look down and see blood streaking your arm, dripping off the sword clutched in your hand. A meadow dotted with yellow flowers lies before you, hacked bodies scattered among the buttercups. Flies are beginning to join the honeybees. The buzzing fills your ears. The hot coppery smell of blood and the reek of death drench you. You search desperately for the body of your sworn enemy, but he is not there.

Your sight flickers again, and you are on a high cliff overlooking a gelid grey ocean. A baby complains at your breast. You search the horizon, but the ship which sailed away with your husband is nowhere in sight. Salt air stings your skin. Despair fills your heart. You struggle to remember why, but all you can feel is the desire to cradle the baby closer to you and step into the air.

You open your eyes and gaze into the face of your beloved. Her mouth tastes of honey and salt. You ripple together. For a moment it feels as if you have sunk into her gleaming black skin and melded with her into a single quivering flesh.

A scream rips you out of your frozen terror. You peek down from your hiding place in the hayloft and see your mother jerking under the body of a Saxon invader. Your father hangs, spinning, watching from where they have hoisted him. Your older brother lies nearby, his viscera gleaming beside him. Your sisters have been dragged off. You can still hear them, though. From the bottom of the ladder a bearded face looks up at you, splits into a yellow grin. He begins to climb.

A soft muzzle lips your palm. You stare in wonder at the pony, the color of honeycomb, its creamy forelock falling over its eyes. Its warm hide smells of sunshine and grass and wonder. "Mine?" you whisper, looking up at your daddy. He smiles down at you, so much love in his face. "Yours," he says, and your heart overflows.

You stare out at the field stretching before you under the hot sun. It is full of stones. You look down at the plough, already warped and bent, and the drooping head of your ox. Weariness pulls at you, tries to sink you into the earth like the seeds you scatter in the thin dust. If your hungry children were not waiting for you, you would lie down and be done.

You tumble through the lives, so many lives. You are battered, exhausted, wracked with agony, pierced with terror, drowned in scents, submerged in carnal bliss, shaking with laughter, lonely and overwhelmed and sated and starving, hurled into death and dragged into life. You fight to find yourself in all of your selves. Finally you surrender. A welcome darkness takes you.

Pain flashes in your finger. You peel one eyelid open and see the raven near your hand, his beak cocked. You notice that your hand is lying on soft green turf, and the mellow sunshine lies gently upon you again. You manage to move your head.

A woman sits a few feet away. She is not looking at you. She is braiding daisies into a chain, head bent, intent on her task. You blink, trying to focus on her, but she shimmers, the sunlight seeming to bend away from her.

The raven gives your finger another sharp peck, then flutters over to her and perches on her shoulder. She strokes it absently.

"Who are you?" you croak, your voice as harsh as the raven's. The woman glances at you and stands, brushing away the loose petals and stems from her thin gown. Taking a step toward you, she offers a hand. You take it and she pulls you to your feet. You stand in the grass facing each other.

She is much, much taller than you. Her skin is the color of rich new earth, her hair the deep luminous black of a moonless sky. Her eyes are startling, pale and bright. There is movement in their depths, secret and dangerous. She takes the daisy chain, twists it into a garland and places it on your head. She says nothing.

"All those lives," you whisper finally. "It's too much. It's too terrible. How can I bear it?"

Those pitiless eyes meet yours. "You thought Memory was a kindness?" She snorts. "All those other times you chose the waters of Lethe. If you wanted comfort, you should have done so again."

"I didn't know," you reply. "I didn't remember."

"No," she says. The raven stirs on her shoulder. "Now your choices will be very different."

She turns and walks away, trailing the scent of smoke and oleander and graveyards.

"What happens now?" you call after her. "What should I do?"

She fades into the trees, becoming diaphanous, and finally disappears. The raven hovers for a moment disconsolately, then flaps away, deeper into the garden.

Mnemosyne, Goddess for the Ages

by Tom Cabot

Remember Mnemosyne, among the old Gods.
    — Nonnos, *Dionysiaca* 31.186[1]

Within the totality, the living animal that is this universe[2], to re-member a thing is to reassemble that which has been dis-membered. Certainly a prototypical mythical instance of this can be found in the Rig Vedic hymn 10.90, known also as the *Purusha Sukta*. In this hymn the primordial human (purusha) is sacrificed by unnamed beings, which I like to think of as Gods. By the end of the hymn this

---

[1] I have modified the translation of the Greek text for effect. Nonnos was a 5th c. Egyptian poet, born in Panopolis, in the same century as Proclus, the late Platonic systematizer of pagan Theology. While Proclus was a truly great interpreter of the Homeric and Orphic Gods, Nonnos' *Dionysiaca*, filled with rhetorical flourishes, was a fanciful and unreliable account of Greek myth, even though, as H. J. Rose has said, "... the searcher into sundry odd corners will be rewarded for his pains ..."

[2] The Living Animal that is this Universe has a paradigmatic source among the Intelligible Gods in Proclus' *Theology*, the Living Animal Itself, *to autozoon*, understood to be the Orphic Phanes, but sometimes called the universal paradigm, the living source of all living things. See Jan Opsomer in Wright 2000, Proclus on Demiurgy and Procession in the *Timaeus* 113-143, esp. n. 31, 135.

is said to be the sacrifice sacrificing to itself. The various parts of Purusha become the various parts of the physical world, the four quarters, sun, moon, various animals and elements, as well as the orders of society, workers, merchants, warriors, priests, etc. And once we realize that the sacrificial animal's spirit ascends as a part back to the divine whole in order to return benefit to the dismembered world we find that the sacrificial rites are theoretically parallel to the concept of reincarnation. All of physical existence then is in essence, even though most often unrealized as such, a sacrificial process; a fracturing of divine wholes through the prisms of space and time. But if we see Purusha as equivalent to the Living Animal instead of Man, which certainly fits in with the sacrificial myth[3], then we have a mythical representation of what becomes later a metaphysical scheme of emanation from unity to multiplicity (and back again from many to one), as

---

[3] It is the Horse in the *Brihad Aranyaka Upanishad*, for example, whose parts become disbursed to form the physical world.

is found in both Indian and Greek philosophies[4]. The theme occurs in many other mythologies throughout the ancient world, such as the Dionysian myths[5] as well as the Egyptian myth of Osiris remembered by Isis, myths which are equally amenable to similar interpretations. So, to invoke Mnemosyne at the beginning of an epic poem such as the *Dionysiaca* is to request the presence of the Goddess in order to reconstruct and unify the scattered fragments of the story. Thus Nonnos begins, "Tell the tale, Goddess ..." reminiscent of Homer's epic invocation "Tell me Muse ..." The use of the singular term thus implies Mnemosyne as the original unity of the Muses[6].

In a 1968 book, *Bending the Bow*, in a poem entitled "Tribal Memories," Robert Duncan also invokes the Goddess.

---

[4] See Salustius *Concerning the Gods and the Universe* XVI for the Greek conception of the sacrifice as well as for the parallel spiritual and theological significance of the verbal practice of prayer. Also Bernard Dietrich, *From Knossos to Homer* 1-13, in Lloyd 1997, who talks about the ancient celebrations of fertility and rebirth, "the most efficacious" of which "was the act of blood sacrifice which had as its primary aim the release of the powers of renewal ..." Thus the double axe, Labrys, served as both instrument of sacrifice and symbol of renewal.

[5] Sarah Iles Johnston gives an overview of the Orphic myths of Dionysus in Graf and Johnston 2007, 66-93.

[6] Discussion in Athanassakis and Wolkow 206.

Mnemosyne, they named her, the
      Mother with the whispering
feathered wings.   Memory,
the great speckled bird who broods over the
      nest of souls, and her egg,
    the dream in which all things are living.

Mnemosyne is not only the unifying force of the poetic mind but in Her is also recollected the elements of reality. In Orphic Hymn 77, 2nd to 4th c. CE, Mnemosyne is She "who gives coherence / to the mind and soul of mortals". This relatively late hymn begins

    I call upon queen Mnemosyne
      Zeus' consort,
who gave birth to the holy,
      the sacred, the clear voiced Muses.

Great Zeus in Greek myth represents the liminal point between the old Gods and the new. To Socrates in the Cratylus, however, the transition from Titan to Olympian Gods in Hesiod's *Theogony* was not even mentioned and the old Gods, Ouranos, Kronos, Hestia, etc. were treated equally with the new. In later Platonic thought Kronos and Rhea were still primary deities, as they were in Orphic texts. In modern thought we might interpret the myths of Titanic progressions either psychologically or as transferences of power from older religious dispensations to newer. Or, as especially in the case of Aphrodite, as generative of orders of the Real. Such myths are, after all, devised by humans. Historically Ouranos and Gaia (Ge) were primordial Gods at the beginning of time when the separation of the powers of earth and sky was realized. This was also the case for the Vedic poets where the sky God *Dyaus pita* (father sky) is always found paired with the mother *Prithivi*. These Gods give the essential shape of reality to the human mind, earth and sky with space itself between. This order of the physical realm later becomes the Demiurgic creation in Plato's *Timaeus*: The two primary creative Gods, Zeus and Ge (in conjunction with Hephaestos, fire, a lower Demiurge) are the foundational creators and space becomes the Nurse of Becoming, the Receptacle of Meaning (Form), in between. In Proclus' 5th c. Platonic Theology[7] Kronos is the primary deity, or pure Intellect in the Intellectual or creative order while Rhea is second as the Life-giving principle. Zeus then is the third deity, the Demiurgic Creative Mind. Of course we know that the Sanskrit *Dyaus* is cognate with the

---

[7] There is a useful graph outlining all this at the end of Duvick's translation of Proclus' *Commentary on Plato's Cratylus*. The Orphic order of theological, or cosmological, transitions runs from Uranus to Kronos to Zeus and finally end up with the reign of Dionysos, Graf and Johnston 2007, 66.

Greek Zeus[8], and it is very likely that this God, however named, is very old. While the Rig Veda is said to be the beginning of what is now called Hinduism, the RV collection of poetic hymns is actually the end result of an at least centuries-long, if not longer, tradition of poetical practice preceding it, and it seems likely that the origins of these practices extend back to the time before the Greek and Vedic peoples separated[9], eventually migrating to their respective home lands. At any rate, the Greek myths give us the reign of Zeus as a transitional period.

In many myths it seems to be here that Mnemosyne is disbursed into what at first was three and then later nine Muses. In many stories Zeus lay with Mnemosyne for nine nights and after a year She gave birth to nine muses, but this myth seems to be a merely explanatory reinforcement for the Homeric cults of the Olympian Gods. Zeus, we

------

[8] Walter Burkert, *From Epiphany to Cult Statue: Early Greek Theos,* in Lloyd 1997 15-34 gives a thorough account of the linguistic evidence.

[9] Many scholars posit a Greco-Aryan culture that formed at some point preceding the migrations (e.g., see M. L. West *Indo-European Poetry and Myth*, Oxford 2007), which perhaps moved, respectively, south and westward through Thrace and/or down into Anatolia on the one hand and eastward through what is now Kazhakstan and then south, also ultimately into Anatolia from that direction, and east into the seven rivers system of the Indus valley in what is now Pakistan.

must remember, was originally a Titan Himself, and there are wolf forms of Him found in Zeus Lykaos, as with Apollo Lykaos the Wolf-God, which indicate a very old presence of the God in the human world[10]. As for Mnemosyne and the Muses there are many myths, of the latter sometimes three and at other times nine. The three Muses were mostly seen in terms of poetic practices such as "practising", "remembering", and "singing" while the nine in some Zeus myths were seen as the Ladies mostly of music, various elements of singing and dancing, associated with the Graces and Charities, as well as with the Sirens. But other attributions show them to be more broadly associated with forms of learning: history as well as flute playing, comedy, elegy and tragedy as well as the lyre and dancing, and story-telling and astronomy as well as heroic song. These disciplines and sociological orders are all generated by the mathematical orders in the World Soul, the Sirens being an interesting example, in Plato's account of souls and Soul in bk. 10, 617a, of the Republic. In this mythological account the Sirens are situated on eight circles created by the spindle turning in the lap

---

[10] This and the following can be found in Kerenyi 2000, 103-105. Of course, these original Indo-European cultures were likely influenced by the farther north cultures that initiated the Uralic language families, and through Anatolian associations Semitic influences were also present.

of Necessity (Ananke[11]). The spindle winds the threads that supply the three Fates, the daughters of Ananke, with the material for their tapestries of destiny, past, present and future, spun for descending souls. Thus the singing Ladies form the archetypal octave for the famous music of the spheres, which in the physical realm guides the planets through their fateful cycles.

This broad cultural sense of the Muses was taken farther in *Orphic Hymn* 76 where they are said to be "mistresses of the mind's power"[12] who taught sacred rites and mysteries to mortals. On this track Pythagoras adopted the Muses for philosophic inspiration and the philosopher thus becomes their servant. This inspiration becomes a form of divine possession and *mania*, madness, since it elevates him or her toward divine Symmetry[13]. Plato called

---

[11] Ananke as a Titan is sometimes paired with Kronos and also sometimes called Adrastea, one of Zeus' nurses. Much on Her in the Orphic texts can be found in M. L. West 1983.

[12] On this attribution see Athanassakis and Wolkow, 205 note to line 7 and further commentary on Mnemosyne and Orphic eschatology 206- 207. The Orphic Hymns as we have them "are likely to have been used by an actual community" as they often refer to rituals, officials, and participants "in the cult." Anne-France Morand, Orphic Gods and Other Gods, 169-181 in Lloyd 1997.

[13] Berg 2001, 208 & 210, commenting on Proclus' Hymn III. To the Muses.

philosophy the greatest music because it causes our spiritual powers to bring into harmony the physical world and the ordered motions of the soul[14]. Personally, however, once understood I think all music, as well as knowledge, can condition our remembrance of our Soul life. Both metaphysical and mythological accounts can also work this way, since rational discourse, the means of written philosophy, and the suggestiveness of poetical accounts are only capable of partial explanations of the totality of the Real, requiring that we see beyond the texts themselves.

Another title for the Muses was Mneiai, a plural for Mnemosyne[15], so it is reasonable to see the Muses as the forms of mental and artistic endeavor scattered throughout human society, recollected in the Goddess Mnemosyne Herself. And in the way of mystic rites and the after-life adventures of the individual soul, the first in the collection of the Bacchic gold tablets[16] begins "This is the work of Mnemosyne ..." As the soul journeys along one is advised to seek Mnemosyne's famous Lake, rather than the Lake of Forgetting (Lethe), and while standing before it say "I am a child of Earth (Ge) and starry Sky (Ouranos)". Also in

---

[14] Duvick 100.

[15] Kerenyi 104, also Athanassakis and Wolkow 206.

[16] In Graf and Johnston.

Proclus' hymn To the Muses he admonishes the souls wandering in this life to make use of "immaculate rites from intellect-awakening books" which would teach them

> to strive eagerly to follow the track leading
> beyond the deep gulf of forgetfulness, and to
go pure to their kindred star[17]

This all takes us back to Mnemosyne and Her ancient origins as a daughter of Gaia and Ouranos, and I see no reason not to accept Her as an essential divine power in contemporary practice as well. True, there are not many ancient accounts of cult practice for Mnemosyne, but by rights she is present in, while sanctifying, all ritual and literary work and just as with other Titan Goddesses like Hekate and

---

[17] Berg 209, lines 5-7.

Metis[18] She spans our time from the most ancient to our modern moments.

---

[18] Metis was of course the actual mother of Athena. Zeus impregnated Her before swallowing Her. So She gave birth to Athena within (the cult of?) Zeus, giving Him an intense headache. Hephaestos then had to alleviate the pain by spliting the God's head open with an axe. Out of the fissure Athena arose. There is therefore a direct line of development from Oddyseus, the archetypal *metic* or oracular human, "the traveller, the shaman, magician, and founder of cults," (Burkert in n. 6 above, p. 17), through Athena who always looks after him, back to Metis Herself.

Works Cited

Athanassakis, Apostolos N., and Benjamin M. Wolkow. 2013. *The Orphic Hymns*. Baltimore: Johns Hopkins Press.

Berg, R. M. van den. 2001. *Proclus' Hymns, Essays, Translations, Commentary, Philosophia Antiqua*. Leiden: Brill.

Duncan, Robert. 1968. *Bending the Bow*. New York: New Directions.

Duvick, Brian. 2007. *Proclus, On Plato's "Cratylus"*. Ithaca: Cornell.

Graf, Fritz, and Sarah Iles Johnston. 2007. *Ritual Texts for the Afterlife, Orpheus and the Bacchic Gold Tablets*. New York: Routledge.

Hesiod. 2006. *Theogony, Works and Days, Testimonia*. Translated by Glenn W. Most, *Loeb Classical Library 57*. Cambridge: Harvard University Press.

Kerényi, Karl. 1979. *The gods of the Greeks*. New York: Thames and Hudson.

Lloyd, Alan B. , ed. 1997. *What is a god? : studies in the nature of Greek divinity*. London: Duckworth.

Nock, Arthur Darby. 1988. *Salustius, Concerning the Gods and the Universe*. Hildesheim: Georg Olms. Original edition, Cambridge University Press 1926.

Nonnos. 1984. *Dionysiaca*. Translated by W. H. D. Rouse. 3 vols, *Loeb Classical Library*. Cambridge: Harvard University Press. Original edition, 1940.

Taylor, Thomas. 1994. *Collected Writings on the Gods and the World*. Vol. 4, *The Thomas Taylor series*. Frome, Somerset, UK: Prometheus Trust.

West, M. L. 1983. *The Orphic poems*. Oxford: Clarendon Press.

West, M. L. 2007. *Indo-European poetry and myth*. Oxford: Oxford University Press.

Wright, M. R., ed. 2000. *Reason and necessity: essays on Plato's Timaeus*. London: Duckworth.

<u>O Metis, Grant Your Wisdom Well</u>

by Alexeigynaix

Wise Metis, You Who gave birth to
Athena, Who in war excels,
and in crafts She learned from You:
O Metis, grant Your wisdom well.

Bright Metis, You Who counsel Zeus
and hidden in His belly dwell,
You Whose words are least abstruse:
O Metis, grant Your wisdom well.

Shrewd Metis, You Whom Kronos found
no ally, Who connived that He expel
all Rhea's children Whom He'd bound:
O Metis, grant Your wisdom well.

Sage Metis, You Who must have known
what — counterfactual — befell
Your second child, Who took Zeus' throne,
O Metis, grant Your wisdom well.

Memory Aids Wisdom
by Alexeigynaix

A Prayer to Mnemosyne

by Rachel Iriswings

Hear me, Mnemosyne, ancient Prophetess,
fair-robed; She Who shapes language,
Whom we invoke before every test,
every speech, every email;
Overseer of history, record-Keeper, Poetess,
She Who presides over traditions of the voice,
Symbol of our evolution, Persevering One

With Your blessing, we can praise the Gods
With Your presence, we honor the past
and carry forward the ancient practices
that provide wise counsel
With Your guidance, we spread creative ideas,
news of events, and stories of heroes

With Your help:
I am considerate
my words are carefully chosen
my thoughts remain when my memory fails
Allow me to aid Your work
with my mind, my pencil, keyboard,
the books that bear prayers like these

I admire You, Muse-mother!
I thank You, Mnemosyne!

<u>Prayer to Mnemosyne I</u>

by Rebecca Buchanan

Memory
Mother of Art and Song
Who bears the cup of inspiration:

guide my pen

<u>Prometheus</u>

by John Muro

Oh body be
Breaking,
Breast
Bearing
Wings wrought
In bronze
Burnish,
Cradled in
Feathered
Whirl of pour.
Unbound,
Unblemished;
Bent
Buckled
Blown
Breathlessly
And bare,
Blazing thru
Bottomless
Blue in
Free fall
Wrangling the
Sacred
Sublimity
Of blessed light
From
Heaven.

Prometeo scende dal cielo per dare il fuoco
by Carlo Spiridione Mariotti

<u>Remembering Metis</u>

by Rachel Iriswings

I speak now of the consumed Titan-Nymph,
the Counselor Who lives on through Zeus,
Who aided Him and aids Him still
and therefore aids us all,
savior of the children of Kronos,
and the first mother of grey-eyed Athena

Let us never forget You, Metis,
let us recognize Your wisdom's reach,
and let us honor Your cunning and prudence!

Selective Memory

by Gerri Leen

Mnemosyne lay in the meadow grass, listening to her daughters' laughter. Nine muses, their voices raised in song, free from care. Except for Melpomene. But she could even make tragedy a sweet thing.

Mnemosyne remembered tragedies that weren't even hers. And they were never sweet.

She noticed a peacock strutting down the far side of the meadow and felt dismay come over her. Not now. Not today.

The bird let out a harsh cry.

She saw Clio running across the grass; her daughter waved to her.

The bird cried again, the sound impatient, so Mnemosyne got up and walked to it.

Its voice was no prettier than its cry. "My mistress needs your assistance."

"Why today?" The sun was so bright, the wind sweetly cool.

"She is waiting."

She could not ignore the call: she was a Titan, but Hera was the queen of the gods. "Fine."

The peacock spread its tail, and the sunlit meadow gave way to a shadowed, misty realm. Hera stood between two rivers, wrapped in a white cloak edged with gold. She motioned for the peacock to leave and it disappeared.

Mnemosyne walked to her river—the river of memory — rolling by stormy and dark. Lethe's river of forgetfulness meandered gently on her other side, light from some unknown source dappling it.

Hera looked up, assessing Mnemosyne. "I need your help."

"I know. This is about *him*?" Him: Zeus. Mnemosyne's lover before he married this beauty who couldn't hold him.

Hera met her eyes, holding her hands out in a helpless gesture. "I've forgotten things. He told me I have. I must have drunk from Lethe."

"If you've forgotten anything, it might have been on your own. The mind can do that. To protect us."

"I'm a god. We don't just forget." Hera knelt down by Mnemosyne's river, cupping her hands to hold the water.

"Why do you need me here? If you wish to drink, do so." She knew how this would go and wanted to be somewhere else.

Hera drank. Her expression did not change; she seemed to be waiting for something. Then she laughed — a forced expulsion of air rather than sound. It sounded almost … helpless. "I can't remember."

Mnemosyne moved closer, sinking to the ground next to Hera, feeling the cool mist rise up around her. "If it is in you to remember, my river would have found the memory."

"It was part of me, once. Zeus told me it was."

"What is it you wish to remember?" But she knew. This was part of the game.

"I want to remember what it was like to love him without the anger I feel now. Without the pain of betrayal."

"Perhaps you've never loved him the way you want to remember?"

"Perhaps not. I remember only this pain. It hurts worse now than it did before I drank."

Hera's eyes blazed, and a fierce wind came up, blowing water from Mnemosyne's river in great sheets. But Hera couldn't stop it from flowing, couldn't do more than momentarily lower the level. Memory would not be denied.

Lethe's river began to bubble behind them, and Lethe appeared on the bank, smiling the sinister smile of her mother Eris. "The only way to love a man like Zeus is to start fresh." She held out a goblet that shone with the same strange light of Lethe's river.

Hera eyed the offered gift. She seemed to be remembering something. "I've done this before. I've been here before."

Mnemosyne looked down. Hera had been here before. Many times. And each time she called her to witness.

"You knew." Hera stared at her, lovely brown eyes accusing Mnemosyne of betrayals she had never committed.

"I always know."

"You never hated him, did you? You only loved him? You gave him such beautiful children." Hera sounded like the little girl she'd never been allowed to be.

Mnemosyne felt her heart go out to her. Wanted to hold her, to comfort her. But Hera wouldn't want that. Right now, she wanted only the truth.

"I never hated him." But Mnemosyne's love had been fleeting. She'd been blessed in that.

"Here. Drink." Lethe leaned over, the goblet finding its way into Hera's grasp.

For a moment, Mnemosyne thought Hera might not drink, but then she lifted the goblet to her lips. Her face went slack and held the innocence of a child, the expectation of a young woman. Hera blinked and looked around, as if surprised to find herself in Persephone's realm. "Where is Zeus?"

There was a flash of thunder, and he appeared, his beard freshly combed, his breath sweet with mint. "My love."

Hera ran to him, and he wrapped her in a thundercloud and carried her out of the underworld.

"Why?" Mnemosyne had wondered it before, but she'd never asked. She knew why Zeus wanted it, but didn't know why Lethe helped.

"Even discord gets old," she heard Eris whisper, her disembodied voice causing a chill down Mnemosyne's spine. "But to see it start afresh, to feel it take hold — that's a gift I can't enjoy without my daughter's help."

Lethe sighed. "Someday, I'll defy you, mother. I'll take away all her memories so she won't remember loving him at all. She'll finally be free."

"You say that every time," Mnemosyne said. The weight of Lethe's forgotten words settled onto her before they tumbled into her river.

"Do I?" Lethe asked, as she sank back into her own river, a slave to it. But a peaceful one.

Mnemosyne heard Eris's harsh laughter echoing through the mist and wished herself back to the meadow. The sun shone brightly, taking away the chill from Hades. The peacock was gone, and she saw a gold-tipped cloud that rumbled with thunder.

Hera was getting to know her husband again.

"Mother?" Euterpe ran to her, humming a merry tune as she took her hands. "Come sing with us. Do you remember the song Hermes taught us?"

Mnemosyne nodded. There was nothing she could not remember.

Even if she'd rather forget.

***

The wind blew, and Hera stood on the summit of Mount Olympus, looking for Zeus. Far in the distance, she saw a thundercloud with lightning flying across it. Closing her eyes, she concentrated and heard the sound of tinkling laughter and her husband's hearty cries of pleasure.

"Mother?" Hebe's sweet voice sounded from behind her.

"Go away. I want to be alone."

Hebe came to stand next to her and stared out at the cloud. "It's his nature to stray."

"It shouldn't be. Not when we love each other."

"Why do you always act as if it's the first time when he does this so often?"

Hera stared at her. When had Zeus ever done this to her?

Hebe's eyes were full of pity. "Come, let's take your chariot out."

Hera tried to ignore the hurt inside her. She was the Queen of the Gods. She would not cry. "I want to get far away from here."

Hebe led her to the stables and hooked the horses to the gold and silver chariot. Hera stepped onto it, and the horses pranced nervously, then Hebe jumped in beside her, and they were off. They hit the lowlands, and Hera slashed the reins, sending the horses in the opposite direction from where Zeus hid in the clouds.

The forest gave way to scrub, the green turning to tan. Hera stopped the chariot at a crossroads and felt a familiar shudder take her as she entered Hecate's realm.

Hebe seemed to shrink in on herself, her normal vivacity squelched in this dying land. "I don't like it here."

Handing the reins to her daughter, Hera jumped off the chariot, landing with a puff of dust, scattering scorpions and serpents.

"You." Hecate sat on a rock, her weathered skin, tan robe, and dun-brown hair blending into the desert. She rose, the trailing hem of her robe leaving a current of dust in her wake. "You don't tend to frequent the crossroads unless you want something."

Hera tried to remember if she'd been here before? She had no recollection of coming to this place, but something in her memories felt incomplete.

Hecate pressed her hand against Hera's forehead, then dropped it hastily and gave Hera a look full of disgust — and pity. "What we do to ourselves for love."

"I don't understand."

"No," Hecate said, walking away. "I know you don't."

"I did not give you leave." But as she said it, Hera had to suppress another shudder. She might be the Queen of the Gods, but Hecate was something else — something older.

"Mother, come away." Hebe frowned, her young beauty shining like a white flower in the desert.

Hera knew she'd once been as fresh as Hebe, before she'd born children to Zeus, before her hips had grown rounded and her breasts full and heavy. She glanced at Hecate and thought she saw three faces where there'd been one before. A crone, a young girl, and a woman such as herself, ripe with possibility.

"Why do you give away all that you are?" Hecate clapped her hands, and a line of scorpions and spiders followed her as she walked away.

"What did she mean?" Hebe asked as she took Hera's hand to guide her into the chariot.

"I don't know. But I know who will." Hera took the reins, leaned toward the horses, and whispered, "Mnemosyne."

They raced back over the desert, onto land that grew green and lush. Mnemosyne was alone, lying in a meadow watching the birds fly overhead, turning slowly to watch Hera drive up. She stood, staring at Hera in what looked like surprise. "My queen."

Hera left Hebe in the chariot and crossed her arms to keep warm in a breeze gone suddenly chill. "I have forgotten something."

"Yes?" Mnemosyne looked nervous.

"I'm sure of it. Just as I think I've been here before."

"Here? In this field?"

"Here. At this moment of choice."

Mnemosyne sighed. Then she nodded.

"Take me to your river."

"Hera, I — "

"Take me to your river. At once."

They were suddenly there, standing in a place between two rivers. Lethe's waters of forgetfulness, so clear and sweet looking. And Mnemosyne's river of remembering, the water stormy with lost truths.

Hera didn't hesitate. She knelt and drank.

The truth hurt. It stung like the barbs of a million tiny bees attacking her heart. Memories flooded her, and she slammed her hand down on the water, causing a huge surge to wash over her and Mnemosyne before it ran into Lethe's river.

Lethe screamed, rising from the waters as if burned. "You," she said. "You're early."

"I am years too late."

And Lethe smiled. A secret, scary smile, and somewhere in the darkness, Hera heard a scream.

"My mother will be so displeased," Lethe said, laughing.

"I did this for him." Hera stared at the river that had given her happiness in the emptiness of forgetting. "But no longer."

With a thought, she was in the field, striding toward Hebe, who stared at her and said, "Mother, you're crying."

"No. I'm not." Hera wiped her eyes savagely. She wasn't crying. She would never cry again.

Turning for home, she let the horses pick their way up Mount Olympus.

Zeus was waiting on one of the balconies. "My darling," he said, taking her in his arms.

It had only been a few weeks since she last drank Lethe's water. It had taken him so little time to get tired of her.

She let him hold her one last time. Then she whispered, "You smell of wood nymphs. Of demigoddess. Of humans. Of swans and lovely, willowy creatures who you should not touch. You reek of all of them, my husband. And you make me sick."

He let her go. "And you reek of Mnemosyne's river."

"You prefer I stink of Lethe's?" Backing away from him, she held her head high. "I can't stop what you do. I can't make you a different man. But I can choose what I know and what I don't."

"Hera—"

"No. I choose, not you. And I choose to remember everything."

For a moment, he seemed to be considering ways to win her back. His smile was fixed in place and he held his hand out to her.

"I choose."

The smile faded, and she saw his true face. His voice was harsh and low as he said, "You won't like living this way."

"You're no doubt right."

The look he gave her was full of hatred, and she imagined it always would be.

She found she could live with that.

Themis and Phoebe

by Rachel Iriswings

The ancestry of oracles is ancient and deep,
highlighted by Delphi: place of prophecy
The will of the Fates has many voices

Order and Light meld to Truth:
dew on the web of possibility
hangs heavy over probability
To brush it over the eyelids
is to receive a gift
and a command
Our voices, Their words

Senses shut down
let the inner voice scream
Intuition made manifest
Ceremonial breaths
Flickers in the dark
Dewdrops beckon

Unwrap the banners from our ears,
raise them in the temple again

the Fates have never whispered

Titanic Spirituality: The Aeon of Saturn

by Darius Matthias Klein

We live in an age of manifestation: the tangible, the quotidian, the personal, the immediate — these are the hallmarks of contemporary consciousness, seemingly tailor-made to meet the exigencies of our zeitgeist. In such existential circumstances, the human psyche naturally inclines toward confession, revelation, and a dogmatic adherence to the Truth. The cosmic cycle of Death and Rebirth has made the fatal round to the domain of the latter, which has now become historic fact — Aphrodite, like Mary the Jewess synthesizing the Philosopher's Stone in her laboratory, has reassembled the limbs and members of Adonis into a coherent whole once more, and the latter takes his leave of his entombment within the bowels of the Earth, sallying forth in the light of the Sun at morning, bearing its blinding rays as a diadem upon his guileless, guiltless brow, and proclaiming all the while the Wisdom that, having originated in the universal, protophanic intellect pervading the cosmos, is now the birthright of humankind. Perception and reality have merged, the Lords of the Heavens have banished falsehood according to the ancient covenants, declaring through the words of their hierophants of old that it was blasphemy to avoid the judgment, a perverse and nihilistic bid to the senescence of the previous epoch, for the renewal for which all had yearned throughout the ages was finally at hand!

Such is the *Jovian Aeon* — the reign of Jupiter — in which we live, an imperial age by any account. Yet there is another generation, another lineage of the spiritual realm, the generation that deploys its powers of scrutiny in another fashion altogether: I speak of course of the *Saturnian Aeon* — the reign of Saturn, Lord of the Titans, the gods of the primordium, the beginnings of all things. The Aeon of Saturn is indeed a more ancient lineage than that of Jupiter, as all of the cosmological accounts of the ancients verify for us. It is the aeon of Earth, mingling with Water; it communicates directly with the Abyss, mediating between it and the incarnate world. According to the mystics of the school of Athens, Kronos - the name by which the Greeks denoted Saturn (the latter being the Roman name) - receives the knowledge of the cosmos and all things which it contains in a cyclical, ever-renewing fashion from Preexistence (*Chaos* to the Greeks, *Numma* to the Sumerians, along with the *Divine Ogdoad* of the Egyptians), while his female emanation, Rhea, whom the Greeks allegorized as his wife (for Kronos, like all the Titans, was hermaphrodite), fashions the souls in which this knowledge will subsist; when Kronos and Rhea re-unite in hypostatic ecstasy, they engender Phorcys, anthropoid sea-scorpion of the fevered Roman *décadence*, image of the Abyss mirroring its fearsome, delectable, substanceless substance; and Phorcys in turn brings forth the souls into the aeon of incarnation.

The Greek poets allegorized this process by depicting Kronos-Saturn as the benign king of a precedent Golden Age, an ante-historical epoch of innocence and plenty, subsisting midway between pure intellection and incarnation, lost to the view of those of us living in the realm of matter which had somehow (d)evolved from it, and to which we now regard as the object of wistful longing, only fleetingly perceptible in dreams, or recalled in the images of the most inspired poets.

The Saturnian Aeon does not, therefore, call its own from among the mass of humankind: rather, it engenders their souls from the primordial stew, as it were, the transmutation of which the ancients denominated *Alchemical*, in its prototypical sense, that its awesome numinescence, its occult splendor, never be lost. This is the origin of the Saturnian lineage in the human race.

The Saturnian Aeon presides over the following:

Among metals, gold, corresponding to his middle state between Pre-Existence and Incarnation. As the Saturnian Aeon presides over all that is Earthy, the igneous stone of volcanic eruptions and, indeed, the pyroclastic seas forever roiling in the bowels of the Earth retain much Saturnian virtue in their substance, whether they lie beneath the ocean's waves or above it. The fossils of biota from prehistoric epochs are particularly potent with regard to this same virtue.

Among the entirety of the kingdom of plants, *Cannabis* and *Opium* are perhaps the most quintessentially Saturnian, conducive as they are to visions of an ineffable Paradise. The same can be said for those representatives of the Fungi which, arising from the Earth as if they were tangible tokens of its essence, contain psilocybin or other chemical properties advantageous for various forms of inter-psychic resonance. Plants species with ancient lineages which rise up from the ooze, such as horsetails or skunk cabbage, are peculiarly Saturnian; in fact, swamps, bogs, fens, marshes, morasses — the Saturnian Aeon presides over all of them and the creatures they contain, inasmuch as they replicate, as much as possible, the undifferentiated primordial environment whence arose all of the living forms.

In addition to swamps and morasses, there are other places, often having long been the sites of religious pilgrimage, which are by definition Saturnian: ruins, cyclopean monuments, cavities in the Earth, *etc*. Because of Kronos-Saturn's association with all that is primitive or primordial, the semi-mythical prehistoric civilizations of Atlantis and Lemuria are Saturnian. The cultic practices of Stone Age humankind — serpent worship (ophiolatry), ancestor veneration, the manipulation of elemental spirits, the conception of the soul as a winged, serpentine entity — are perforce Saturnian.

Of the animals, the Saturnian include serpents, toads, scorpions, and moles — such creatures as maintain their habitations in subterranean zones, or those, as just mentioned, which flourish in those richly biodiverse environments where Earth and Water flow together inextricably. According to the ancient Greeks, serpentine birds who dwell in such places, such as the heron, and most especially the ibis - the emblem of the god Thoth, revered by the Egyptians for his wisdom — are among the most Saturnian of the "feathered tribes"; the Egyptians also revered the snake-necked goose as emblematic of the primordial chthonic god *Geb*, whom the Greeks equated with Kronos-Saturn himself. Those animals we denote as "living fossils" — horseshoe crabs, the contemporaneous cousin of the trilobites untold millions of years ago, or the impossibly long-lived sharks of the shadowy oceanic abyss, practically unchanged since the dawn of time, subsist in the Saturnian Aeon; of all the past epochs of the Earth, the hothouse, luxuriantly swampy hothouse world of the *Carboniferous*, most bears the Saturnian mark. Nocturnal animals, such as the sagacious owl, or gentle but mysterious opossum, are likewise Saturnian.

Of magical rites, those pertaining to the earthen and watery spirits, blood sacrifice, or communication with the dead, are Saturnian. Those rites intended to influence perception, so that the operant may cause the subject to behold with the carnal eye those things which are part of the invisible, spiritual world, did the Saturnian philosophers of old formulate for those whom the crass material world had rendered effete. The hekatic rites of the Egyptian sages, whether they be those inscribed on the sarcophagi of the most ancient pyramids, or the exquisitely abstruse procedures of natural magic and theurgy which the first Hermetists pioneered, are the most efficacious, and most openly bear the primordial Saturnian stamp of any national tradition. But the *pièce de résistance* of Saturnian magic is undoubtedly the artificial creation of life, such rites by which the operant aligns their will, and hence becomes like unto, the elemental entities responsible for the primordial generation of the first living forms, the bacterial soups of the earliest epochs. In keeping with their Saturnian nature, procedures of this kind are occult in the extreme, and suitable only for the doughtiest of operants.

Children of the Saturnian Aeon — those whom Phorcys first plucked from the invisible realm, as mentioned above — are pensive and melancholic: hence, the familiar term *saturnine*. Prone to brooding and not averse to cultivating suitably mysterious personae, Saturn's children are nevertheless no flighty dilettantes: they are those who work their *heka* in secret, divulging the nature and outcomes of their operations to no one, nor feeling any need to do so. Their eschewal of the flashy, the ingratiating, the tinsel, the tawdry, usually renders them invisible to the loud, clamoring rabble of ordinary humanity — a blessing in their eyes, inasmuch as they dread lest that same rabble appropriate, and thereby corrupt, the products of their wisdom. The more recondite occult traditions, such as Gnosticism or Typhonic magic, naturally attract them; they tend to regard the more user-friendly iterations of Wicca and neo-Paganism with a certain air of supercilious condescension. They peruse the oft gruesome recipes of the grimoires with the avidity of a medieval Catholic receiving the Eucharist; the rigorous initiatory demands of the Hermetic traditions, requiring countless hours of ascetic withdrawal for the purposes of study and contemplation, these they find irresistibly alluring, rather than daunting — for the children of the Saturnian Aeon are such as work by night, in order to do that which they must do.

These tendencies arise not from the hardness of their hearts, but from the depth of their inner longing. For those born under the Saturnian Aeon forever ache with a wist for the Golden Age, vanished long ago, when Kronos-Saturn was king, for the wan innocence of the Garden of Hesperides, where flow the fountains of perpetual youth, in an unceasing upwelling from the bowels of the Earth, the source of all *heka* and wisdom. Their diffident aspect notwithstanding, the inner children of Saturn's spawn may never forget what was lost, for it never ceases to tantalizingly linger, just past the margins of visibility, in the corners of their minds' eyes. The knowledge, moreover, has not escaped them, that it is they who will keep the vision of the lost Paradise alive for ages to come, for they alone can almost see it, almost touch it, almost — through the ancient sciences they alone have mastered — cause it to materialize once more. This is the blessed end which the children of Saturnian Aeon forever seek.

MAY THE BLESSINGS OF THE UNIVERSAL MIND BE YOURS!

To Iapetus

by Ariadne Rainbird

Ancestor of Mankind, mighty Iapetus,
Pillar of the West, the Heavens' support,
Father to Atlas, strongest of strong,
And to Prometheus, God of forethought,
And Epimethius who with his brother,
Crafted mortal creatures out of clay,
Allotting to each creature it's own special gifts
Your mighty sons the Iapelidae,
Then, on to man, who naked roamed
With neither claw, nor horn, nor fang,
With all the blessings now allotted
What after-thought was left for man?
Taking pity on his plight
They gave the gift of craftsmanship.
O Mighty Bearer of the Cosmos
Who dwells in the depths of the Tartarian pit,
Where earth, sea and sky have their roots
The Span of mortal life You allot
Presiding over our baser nature
And giving to each our finite lot.
Mankind inherited all the worst,
Of Your sons' characteristics, so it's told
Sly and crafty, rash and scheming,
Guileless, violent, arrogant, and bold.
To the traits that led each to their downfall,
Let us not submit, but with hearts that are true,

Let us strive for all their best qualities
And transform our vices into virtue.
Bless Your mystics Mighty Piercer,
With Atlas's endurance, Menoetius's might
From Epimethius, to learn from mistakes
And from Promethius Divine Foresight.
Let us rise up from our baseness
And with roots in earth to the heavens reach
Awaken the striving that resides within us
That we may know the mysteries You teach

<u>To Koíos</u>

by Ariadne Rainbird

O Titan God of the questioning mind
Prophetic voice of Your father Sky
And with Shining Phoebe the primal font
Wherein all the knowledge of the cosmos lies
Father to Leto and Asteria, who in turn
Bore children mighty and strong
Apollon who gives prophecies of light and heaven
And Hekate to whom Kthonian powers belong
Titan of intellect, the axis of heaven
Around which the constellations revolve
Lord of the North celestial pole
God of philosophy, enquiry and resolve
Your firey Drakon surrounds heaven's pole
Like the serpent that guarded the naval of earth
The Oracle of Delphi, where Phoebe ruled
Before blessed Apollon's divine birth.
O father of wisdom Mighty Koios
Let Your mystics not be ignorant and blind
Lead us to philosophy's rational eye
May we be inspired by your enquiring mind
To subject all that we think we know
To rational analysis, questioning all
To realise that we who think we know much
In double ignorance know nothing at all
But single ignorance is the key
To the beginning of wisdom when we realise

That we, full of hubris, are indeed ignorant
For only then may we become wise.

❖

*Prometheus and Epimetheus Before Pandora
by Hermann Julius Schlosser*

<u>To Prometheus</u>

by Ariadne Rainbird

Hail far seeing Titan, friend to mankind
Bringer of many gifts, with benignant mind,
Giver of fire and teacher of skills
Saviour of humankind, protector from ills.
Son of Iapetus and Themis wise
Who taught the portion of sacrifice
Thyself sacrificed to aid mankind
Prometheus I call, many skilled, kind
Who in Thy workshop fashioned Alethia
Let truth guide us, Oh wise seer.
Fashioner of men and beasts from the sacred soil
Clay mixed with tears, a token of our toil
Aepymetes, lofty-minded Titan Great
Who gives the power to see our fate
Who shows the paths to freedom and slavery
Guide Thy mystics on the path of the free
The path that begins rough and steep
But ends with repose and understanding deep.
O Wise Prometheus, kindle the fire of my soul
And aid Thy mystic on the path to be whole.

The Underworld

Hekate
by Maximilián Pirner

Epithets of Hekate

by Rachel Iriswings

Split-fingered, three-faced,
She Who watches, guide and guardian,
silhouette at the crossed paths
Who hangs Her lantern on the signpost,
cone of light above the rural road,
ancient halo above the trail,
ageless, Liminal One
Whose hounds sing Her praises in the night,
smoke above the burning beacon,
solemn gaze as dusk falls, lion's eyes,
powerful presence, distant, clouded, veiled
serpentine grace, ominous, wise, esoteric,
robed in red and black and white,
honored under the arcane moon,
remembered in silence and solitude,
intriguing Keeper of magicks,
daughter of Perses Who destroys
and of Asteria of the falling stars,
mother of none, enthroned by gods and mortals,
stern in expression, tender in heart

<u>Hekate and Her Ghostly Retinue</u>

by Rebecca Buchanan

serpent-hair
tiny hisses forked tongues
iridescent greens and blues and purples and such
reds
gown of mist and moonlight and earth-deep
shadows
barefoot down the road
puppy in hand
(left at a crossroad shrine
suffocated
favored offering)
dogs circling her legs
yipping
barking
running ahead and back
circling running again
and the ghosts who follow
uncounted
a river of pain fear denial
angry
hungry for the life never lived
now never to be lived
howling in anguish
answering howl from the dogs
the puppy whines in her hands
serpent-hairs rise and hiss tongues snapping
and the ghosts are silent again
for a moment

Hekate's Domain

by Gerri Leen

Up ahead lies the crossing place
Dusty and lonely
Given over to things that crawl and slither
Rattlers and copperheads, scorpions and centipedes
Hecate's children
Counting off by two

The crossroad's dust masks broken
People kneeling at
The intersection of roads
Making promises they won't
Want to keep to a goddess
Older than they know

Hecate hovers — there
On the stop sign
Lounging on the traffic signal
Go
Stop
Slow down — the most important
Consider what you can afford to pay

She won't linger
So many crossroads supplicants
Only one goddess
Snakes dance goodbye

A bobcat stands frozen like a rabbit
By the dark abyss of her eyes

Crone
Witch
Wise One
Dealmaker
She is all and none of these
She flies on, crows and owls at her side
Ancient enemies except
When they attend their mistress
At the crossroads
Real and imagined

Hekate
by Ariadne Rainbird

Hellenic Hekate Ritual: A Self-Dedication Rite

by Tina Georgitsis

Self dedication to Deity has been constant since the beginning of acts of worship and veneration of the Gods. In the modern world many practitioners self-initiate if choosing to work alone and/or to strengthen their devotion to a specific God/dess.

In Ancient Greece the mythology of Medea shows she was a dedicated Priestess to Hekate. Although much is not known with respects to how or why she dedicated herself to Hekate (some make connections to her as the Daughter of Hekate), she was as a strong willed and capable woman of power, who gained and possessed the knowledge to work with Hekate and honour her. Similarly, Circe who is considered Medea's niece or aunt in Ancient Greek mythology, as well as a daughter of the Gods (like Medea some make connections to her as the Daughter of Hekate), she was also a dedicant to Hekate and was known to be a very powerful sorceress in her own right who was dedicated to Hekate. You can also add Queen Hekabe, Gale and/ or Galinthias as Hekate's devotees who were transformed into animals and adopted by Hekate and turned into her familiars.

It's quite common for witches, magicians and reconstructionists to dedicate themselves to

Hekate as Goddess of Witchcraft, Magic, Moon, Night, Necromacy and Ghosts. Due to being a Hellenic practitioner I have created a simple, yet effective method of dedicating yourself to Hekate with a Hellenic influence which I have shared below:

Hellenic Hekate Self Dedication Ritual
<u>Preparation</u>

Chose a liminal time and place for the ritual to be set.

Purify body by showering or washing head, hands and feet.

Clean and purify your shrine and all items which will be placed on the shrine.

Your shrine items should include: khernips (purified water), barley seeds, asperging herbs (small bundle purifying herbs such as bay leaves), oil lamp or candle, resin incense and incense holder (such as heatproof bowl) and an image of Hekate. Your offering items which can include perishable and non-perishable items.

Create a Dedication of Purpose of Dedicant. This dedication should include the reason for devoting yourself to Hekate and what you will be doing to Honour Hekate ie perform regular magick and ritual in her name, observe her sacred times and holidays and learn more about her and/or share that knowledge.

<u>Ritual</u>

Wash your hands in khernips before standing before your shrine, whilst saying:
Αφήστε όλα αυτά που είναι βλαβερά να φύγουν!
(Let all that is profane be gone!)

Present the offerings to Hekate by holding them up in a gesture of oblation and place them on the shrine. You do not need to speak to do this but may say a few words as a statement of purpose if you are inspired.

Take your asperging herbs and dip into khernips and flick water onto the shrine.

Take a handful of barley and throw them onto the shrine.

When complete say:
Xerniptosai! (Be Purified!)
Light the oil lamp/candle.
Light the incense.

<u>Invocation</u>

Invoke Hekate with a favourite hymn or write one in her name.

Touch your forehead, lips, heart and tap the shrine — repeat three times.

<u>Praxis</u>

Read out your Dedication of Purpose of Dedicant.

Petition of Promise. Read out this Petition of Promise:

Hekate I call to you
That I may serve as your committed dedicant
Whose devotions are made in your name
Hekate I call to you
Bless me as I walk your path
Remove obstacles which may hinder in this task
Hekate I call to you
With faith and active determination
May you dwell in my heart and soul

<u>Thanks and Closing</u>
Thank Hekate by saying:
Hekate, in your name I have devoted myself to you. In your name, may the way open for me to be your dedicant.

Blow out candles and put out incense.

Step away from the shrine by backing away, turning to the right and leaving without looking back.

Ritual is now complete and any feasting can take place.

Illuminating the Path: A Hymn to Hekate

by Tina Georgitsis

Hekate, Mistress of Magic
I come to you as devotee
Hekate, Light Bringer
Illuminate my way in this time of darkness
Hekate, Guide of the Crossroads
Show me the true path of purpose
Hekate, Opener of Doors
Allow me to seek clarity of vision
Hekate, Keeper of the Key
Unlock your mysteries to me

<u>King and Queen of the 'Neath-lands:</u>
<u>An Excerpt</u>
by Alexeigynaix

Sing, Muses, how the Gods first came to be,
each child of Earth and starry Heaven bright.
First Khaos, then the Earth. From Khaos, Night;
from Earth, Her equal, Heaven: He sired Sea,
and other Straining-Gods, with Kronos, key
later. Earth bore Hundred-Handers, Giants' might
that Heaven feared. He locked them from the light
within Earth's lands. Kronos, setting free
(together with His brothers) Mother Earth,
held Heaven by four limbs and by the balls,
which Kronos severed with a flint-knapped knife.
These fell to Ocean — Aphrodite's birth.
Ash-trees sprang up with every blood drop's fall.
Thus Heaven ceased to tyrannize His wife.

[Author's Note: a gift from my fandom identity to AO3 user Apricot in the Once Upon A Fic 2017 fanfiction exchange challenge.]

On the Dark of the Moon

by Suz Thackston

Have you met Hekate?

Maybe Hesiod introduced you to her. He tells of her lineage as a powerful Titan, given dominion over the realms of earth, sea and sky by Zeus himself for her help in overthrowing her fellow Titans and securing the rule of the Olympians.

Maybe you know her as a goddess of witches, patron of famed sorceresses such as Medea and Circe. Shakespeare puts her in charge of his three savage crones, the witches who bring down MacBeth.

Perhaps you've encountered her as a lunar goddess, or a crossroads guardian, or even one of her most important aspects, a psychopompos who shepherds souls to the afterlife when they leave their bodies.

Maybe your encounter goes something like this.

I walk to the three-way crossroad at dusk, on the dark of the moon. It is very quiet in the late winter twilight, pale purple sky and dirty white snow. Two cats pad silently behind me. A big black dog snuffles in the undergrowth next to the road.

I place my offerings in the ditch next to an old wooden post. There are rudimentary faces carved into the post, three of them, each overlooking the direction the road takes. They are very crude, round eyes, slit nostrils, gaping wide mouths. I shiver and try to move where the eyes can't see me, but they follow.

I stand silent for a while as the dusk thickens around me. My dog bumps my knee inquisitively, then wanders away, following a scent trail into the adjoining field. The cats sit on either side of me, silent, motionless.

There is a crack in the woods behind me. The hair on the nape of my neck prickles. I turn slowly. An eight-point stag stands on the verge of the road, watching me. We stare at each other for a full minute. He lowers his head, his horns menacing me, then turns and rubs them, hard, on the bark of an old sycamore tree. The noise is startling in the quiet night, harsh and rasping.

A loud bark interrupts the stag's challenge. The dog comes racing across the field and into the road, stopping next to me, panting loudly. Dog and stag stare at each other. Then the stag leaps back into the woods. The dog starts to follow, but stops at my word and sits next to the post, whining almost inaudibly. Her head whips around and she stares down the road from the west. Something is approaching.

It looks like a streamer of smoke in the near-darkness, wavering, flowing, almost dancing. The dog goes silent, stiff and wide-eyed. The cats move softly to the verge of the woods.

We all watch the procession approach.

First come the small things, mice and toads and voles and chipmunks, scurrying and hopping. They pay no attention to us. Snakes writhe between them. They are followed by slightly larger creatures, rabbits and skunks and possums. They all pause briefly at the post, then turn away down the road to the southeast, unhurried but purposeful. They are all black, and slightly translucent.

I put a hand on my dog's head. She is trembling slightly. I am trembling a lot.

The procession continues with geese and pigs and goats and sheep, all black, all moving with feet that don't quite touch the ground, all pausing for a short moment at the post where I stand with the dog, all passing by us as if we aren't there.

Cows, horses, elk, bears, mountain lions. A big cat casts a glowing eye at the two small ones at the edge of the woods. They tense as if to flee, but as the shadowy beast moves on they remain motionless.

A wraithlike shape approaches me. A black pony with a faintly glowing stripe of white down his face and a cascading mane. He touches me with a muzzle I can't feel, but I know is soft as a petal. Tears stream down my face as he moves on.

Huge things lumber past. Elephants and camels, other things I cannot name. Winged things fly above the procession, dark and silent.

Finally the procession ends. The night is fully dark. I draw in a shuddering breath and turn to leave, but halt when a small noise escapes my dog.

A figure walks toward us out of the west, almost invisible in the enshrouding darkness, a gleam of pale light around its brow. As it draws near, flames erupt from torches held in either hand, a cold, spectral fire.

The goddess Hekate halts before us. My knees give way and I sink into a heap next to the ditch. The dog presses into me, half collapsed in my lap. The cats draw near.

Hekate sets her torches in the ground on either side of the post, where they create a pool of cold pale light. The eyes and mouths of the faces on the post seem to blink and utter silent words.

She leans over the ditch and looks down at the offerings I have set there, hard boiled eggs, cubes of white cheese, a tea bag from the cup of mint tea and honey I have poured. I hold my breath. She straightens and holds out her hand.

I reach slowly into the pocket of my hoodie and pull out a quill pen. I hand it to her, my fingers trembling. She takes it from me and turns it over in her hands. Suddenly she laughs, a surprising sound, high and girlish and joyful. She flourishes the quill high in the air, like a wand, and it leaves a faint glowing trail across the starry sky. Then she stands still. Her face is featureless in the night except for a gleam of eyes. She takes the pen and touches the sharp nib to a fingertip. A silver drop oozes out, shockingly visible despite the darkness.

She holds out her left hand to me, the silver-tipped pen poised in her right. I give her my hand. She touches the tip to my finger and I feel it bite, sharp as a scalpel.

The goddess touches the tiny wound in my fingertip to the matching one on hers. She licks our mingled blood and ichor off her finger, and hands me back the quill pen. She turns to go.

The calico cat makes a sharp, pleading sound. Hekate turns back. Both cats run to her and twine around her legs. She reaches down and strokes their backs. The dog whines, leaps from me and runs to her, throwing herself to the ground, legs in the air. The goddess crouches beside her and rubs her belly.

Then she leaves us.

Links

https://www.theoi.com/Khthonios/Hekate.html
https://sites.google.com/site/hellenionstemenos/
Home/festivals/hekatesdeipnon
https://forestdoor.wordpress.com/2011/06/29/
hekates-deipnon/
https://en.wikipedia.org/wiki/
Hecate#Boundaries_and_crossroads
https://www.youtube.com/watch?v=LAIgKP-bC_A

To Hekate for Hekate's Deipnon

by Ariadne Rainbird

A supper is traditionally made and offered to Hekate at the dark of the moon. The home is cleaned and purified, and the food may be left at a crossroads, or outside the door of the house, the entrance of the house and the road forming a crossroads. In ancient times when meals were left at crossroads, they would provide sustenance for weary and hungry travellers. An alternative in modern times would be to give the meal to the homeless people local to you, if in an urban area, or leave it out for birds and animals if in a rural area.

Hekate I call, Adamantae, Untamed
Epiphanestate Thea, most manifest and famed
You hold the keys of the Kosmos in your hand
Celestial Goddess, ruling sky sea and land
Starborn, Night-wondering, brilliant guide
Enodia, of the crossroads, Agriope, Wild-Eyed
Opener and closer of the Gates
Of Hades and Heaven, Mistress of Fate
Limenoskopos, who in the liminal dwells
At the thresholds of heaven and deepest hell
Agia, Soteira, Kalliste, in saffron veil
Torch-bearing Dadophorus, All-Goddess hail!
Kynokephalos, with Dog-head
Dwelling with the dark hosts of the dead

Buthios, of the depths, Indominatable Queen
Persephone's hand maiden and Goddess supreme
Kynegetis, leader of hounds
Unconquerable Goddess who knows no bounds
Wonderer between the worlds
Who the keys to the mysteries holds
Decked in black, haunting the night
Yet radiant, Aglaos, with brilliant light
Aid us Blessed Goddess to a life that is true
Oh Holy Advocate of Virtue
And steer us on the path that we may be
Worthy to unlock the mysteries

The Anemoi — the four winds, Boreas, Notus, Eurus, and Zephyrus. Sons of Astraios and Eos, grandsons of Eurybia and Krios.

Asteria — the Titaness of night, the night sky, and night-time prophecy. Sister of Leto, aunt of Apollo and Artemis. By Perses, she is the mother of Hekate. She was transformed into the island of Delos, where Leto took refuge to give birth to her children.

Astraios/Astraeus — the Titan of the stars, astronomy, astrology, and the wind. Son of Krios and Eurybia. By Eos he is the father of the Anemoi (the winds) and, in some stories, the stars.

Atlas — the Titan of daring, endurance, strength, and stamina, as well as astronomy. He was eventually released from his obligation to support the heavens, and instead became the guardian of the celestial pillars. Son of Iapetos and Clymene, brother of Prometheus and Epimetheus.

Aura — the Titaness of the breeze. Daughter of Lelantos. She appears in *The Dionysiaca* as the mother of Iacchus by Dionysus.

Clymene/Klymene — the Titaness of fame. By Iapetos she is the mother of Atlas, Prometheus, and Epimetheus.

Dione — the Titaness of the Oracle of Dodona. In some myths, she is the mother of Aphrodite.

Possibly a daughter of Gaea and Ouranos, making her part of the first generation of Titans. In other stories, she is one of the Okeanides.

Doris — the Titaness of the fertility of the ocean, especially rich fishing grounds. One of the Okeanides, a daughter of Okeanos and Tethys. Among her many sisters are Eurynome, Metis, Perseis/Perse, and Styx. By Nereus, she is the mother of the Nerites and Nereids, including Amphitrite (the wife of Poseidon), Galatea, and Thetis (the mother of Achilles).

Eos — the Titaness of the dawn. Daughter of Hyperion, sister of Helios and Selene. By Astraios, she is the mother of the Anemoi (the winds).

Epimetheus — the Titan of afterthought. Son of Iapetos and Clymene, brother of Atlas and Prometheus. He created the animals of the earth, and was later tricked into accepting Pandora as a wife.

Eurybia — the Titaness of mastery of the seas and oceans. Mother of Astraios, Pallas, and Perses, grandmother of Hekate and the Anemoi.

Eurynome — the Titaness of pasturelands and water-meadows, and, by Zeus, the mother of the Charites (Graces). At her ancient sanctuary at the confluence of the Neda and Lymax rivers, she was represented by a mermaid statue. Generally regarded as a daughter of Okeanos and Tethys, making her one of the Okeanides. She cared for the infant Hephaestus after he was cast from the heights of Olympus.

Hekate/Hecate — the Titaness of the night, ghosts, necromancy, and magic. She also has ties to the ocean and dogs. Daughter of Asteria and Perses, niece of Leto, cousin of Artemis and Apollo, aunt of Circe.

Helios/Helius — the Titan of the sun. He sided with the Olympians during the war, and so maintained his position when most of the Titans were cast out. Son of Hyperion and Theia. By the Oceanid Perseis/Perse, he is the father of Aeetes, Circe, and Pasiphae, and grandfather of Medea, Ariadne, and the Minotaur. He is the father of numerous other offspring by various Goddesses, Okeanides, and mortals.

Hyperion — the Titan of the sun, light, and the cycles of day and night. By Theia is the father of Helios, Selene, and Eos.

Iapetos/Iapetus — the Titan of mortality and the life-span. By Clymene, he is the father of Atlas, Epimetheus, and Prometheus.

Koios/Coeus — the Titan of intelligence, and the axis of heaven. By Phoebe, he is the father of Asteria and Leto, grandfather of Apollo, Artemis, and Hekate.

Krios/Kreios/Crius — the Titan of the stars and the constellations. Associated with the constellation Aries (the ram), whose rising marked the start of the new year. By Eurybia, he is the father of Astraios,

Pallas, and Perses, and grandfather of the Anemoi (the winds) and Hekate.

Kronos/Cronus/Cronos — the King of the Titans. By Rhea, he is the father of the six original Olympian Deities. He castrated his own father, Ouranos, at the instigation of Gaea the Earth Mother. After the war between the Olympians and the Titans, he was cast into Tartaros. In some myths, he is later freed by Zeus and given rulership of the Isles of the Blessed in Elysium.

Kybele/Cybele — originally a Phrygian (Anatolian/ Turkish) Goddess of fertility, cities, mountains, and lions. Her cult spread far and quickly. She came to be closely associated with Rhea, as well as the agricultural Goddess, Demeter, and the Egyptian Goddess, Isis.

Lelantos — the Titan of breezes and unseen movement. In *The Dionysiac*a by Nonnus, he is the father of Aura.

Leto — the Titaness of night, stealth, invisibility, and gentleness. Daughter of Koios and Phoebe. Sister of Asteria, aunt of Hekate. By Zeus, she is the mother of Apollo and Artemis.

Metis — the Titaness of good counsel, wisdom, and instinct. An Okeanid, she is the daughter of Okeanos and Tethys, and sister of Doris, Eurynome, Perseis/Perse, and Styx. She allied with Zeus, and created the elixir that forced Kronos to disgorged his children. Later swallowed herself by Zeus, when he discovered that she was pregnant. The resultant child, Athena, emerged instead from the head of Zeus.

Mnemosyne — the Titaness of memory, words, and language. Daughter of Gaea and Ouranos. By Zeus, she is the mother of the Muses.

Okeanides/Oceanids — the three thousand daughters of Okeanos/Oceanus and Tethys. Known for their prophetic abilities, fertility blessings, and wisdom. Among the most well-known are Doris, Eurynome, Metis, Perseis/Perse, and Styx.

Okeanos/Oceanus — the Titan of the world-encircling river. He remained neutral during the war between the Titans and the Olympians, and so maintained his position after the victory of the latter. By Tethys, he is the father of the Potamides (river spirits), Okeanides (fresh water nymphs), and Nephelai (cloud nymphs). Among his most notable offspring are Doris, Metis, Perseis/Perse, and Styx, making him the grandfather of numerous Gods, Goddesses, demi-gods, and heroes.

Pallas — the Titan of warcraft and military campaigning. The son of Kreios and Eurybia, brother of Astraios and Perses. Husband of Styx and, by her, often listed as the father of Bia, Kratos, Nike, and Zelus. In some myths, he was a childhood friend of Athena, who took his name after his accidental death, though this may have been a different Pallas.

Perseis/Perse — an Okeanid, daughter of Okeanus and Tethys. Sister of Doris, Eurynome (mother of the Charites), Metis (the mother of Athena), and Styx. By Helios, she is the mother of Aeetes, Circe, and Pasiphae, and the grandmother of Medea, Ariadne, and the Minotaur.

Perses — the Titan of destruction, excessive heat, burning, and summer drought. Son of Krios and Eurybia, brother of Astraios and Pallas. By Asteria, he is the father of Hekate. Possibly associated with the dog star.

Phoebe — the Titaness of intellect and prophecy, and the Oracle of Delphi before Apollo. Daughter of Gaia and Ouranos. By Koios, she is the mother of Asteria and Leto, and grandmother of Apollo, Artemis, and Hekate.

Prometheus — the Titan of forethought. Son of Iapetos and Clymene, brother of Atlas and Epimetheus. He created humanity while his brother Epimetheus created animals. He later stole fire from heaven and gave it to humanity, for which he was punished by being chained to a mountain while an eagle ate his liver. Over and over, every single day. He was eventually freed by Herakles.

Rhea — the Queen of the Titans, associated with mountains, lions, and cities. Wife of Kronos, and mother of the original six Olympians. She saved her son Zeus and later aided her children in their war against Kronos and the other Titans. Often associated with the Phrygian Goddess, Kybele.

Selene — the Titaness of the Moon. Daughter of Hyperion and Theia, sister of Helios and Eos. By the mortal Endymion, she is mother of the fifty Menai (lunar months). By Zeus, she is sometimes said to be the mother of Pandia (possibly a Goddess of the full moon), Ersa (the dew) and maybe the Nemean Lion fought by Herakles. In other stories, she is the mother of Narcissus, as well as the legendary demi-god poet, Musaeus.

Styx — the Titaness of oaths, and the underworld river that bears her name (Thetis dipped her infant son Achilles into the waters of the Styx in an attempt to make him invulnerable). One of the Okeanides, she is a daughter of Okeanus and Tethys. Sister of Doris, Eurynome, Metis, and Perseis/Perse. By Pallas, she is the mother of Nike (victory), Zelus (zeal, glory), Bia (force, raw energy), and Kratos (strength). Possibly also the mother of Scylla and Echidna.

Tethys — the Titaness associated with underground sources of fresh water, and with nursing and nursing mothers. Daughter of Ouranos and Gaea. Wife of Okeanos, by whom she is the mother of the Potamides (the rivers), the Okeanides (fresh water springs), and the Nephelai (the clouds). Her most notable offspring are Doris, Eurynome, Metis, Perseis/Perse, and Styx. She is the grandmother of numerous Deities and heroes, including the Nereids, the Charites, Athena, Aeetes, Circe, Pasiphae, and many more.

Theia — Titaness of sight and vision, and precious gems and metals. Daughter of Gaia and Ouranos.

By Hyperion, she is the mother of Helios, Selene, and Eos; and grandmother of Aeetes, Circe, Pasiphae, the Anemoi (the winds), and the Menai (the lunar months), as well as many others.

Themis — the Titaness of natural law and the divine order, and the oracles of the earth. Daughter of Gaea and Ouranos. By Zeus, she is the mother of the Horae (the seasons). As Blind Justice, she stands before many courts of law around the world.

Appendix B: Our Contributors

Alexeigynaix lives in the US Pacific Northwest with a librarian, a fount of oddball wisdom; their cat Thea; and (in Thea's opinion) a terrifying dangerous interloper cat. (Zoe has lived here longer than Alex and Thea have, and anyway, Thea shot first.)

Rebecca Buchanan is the editor of the Pagan literary ezine, *Eternal Haunted Summer*, and is an editor of *ev0ke: witchcraft*paganism*lifestyle*. She has released four short story collections and one poetry collection, with a second due later this year. Her work has appeared in a variety of venues, a complete list of which can be found at eternalhauntedsummer.com.

J. K. Bywaters is an award-winning storyteller and author. His work has appeared in various magazines, anthologies, and online. He is currently the sole curator, storyteller, and unorthodox auctioneer of the real-life experimental project known as The Reedmace Project, detailed at reedmaceproject.livejournal.com. He lives with his family near Brightwood, and cordially invites you to follow him on Facebook and Twitter.

Tom Cabot writes: The principle aim in my life, since I was very young, has been to follow out subliminal visions and recognitions, intuitions, dreams, and so on. The subliminal experiences have led me to recognitions of a number of Gods, among other things, and I have learned to trust what is found in the depths of the mind. This trust with its insights then has formed the basis of my spiritual path. Such a path does not come with a paycheck, however, so I have had numerous jobs over the years. Ultimately, I realized that I would not get through my later years that way, so I went back to school, earned a few degrees, and worked in a university library for twenty years.

Tisdale Flannery is an eclectic devotional pagan and writer of stories and songs.

Tina Georgitsis is a regular writer on Kemetic, Hellenic, Witchcraft and occult subjects and has been featured in several books and magazines internationally. Arch Priestess Hierophant in the Fellowship Of Isis (Lyceum of Heka), Hereditary Folk/Hermetic Witch, Initiated Wiccan Priestess, Reiki/Seichim/Sekhem Master, Tarot Councillor (ATA) who has worked professionally as a reader, healer, purveyor of magickal items and teacher of workshops in various metaphysical and occult subjects. For more information go to her blog: https://setjataset.wordpress.com.

Ϫⲓⲙⲟⲩⲥ writes: A Greco-Egyptian pagan for two years, a new priest of Hermes for a month, and a poet since birth from Perry Hall, Maryland. I always try to praise the gods in whatever way I can. I write my hymns in both English and Fayyumic Coptic (though the one in this book is not in Coptic).

Rachel Iriswings has been a polytheist for over a decade. Her poems are also featured in *From the Roaring Deep*, *First and Last*, *The Diviner's Handbook*, and *Shield of Wisdom*.

Darius Matthias Klein opted not to provide a biography.

Sophia Kouidou-Giles was born in Thessaloniki, Greece, and resides in the USA. With a BA in psychology and an MSW in social work, she has published articles in child welfare journals. A poem from her chapbook *Transitions and Passages* was shortlisted in a juried competition. Her short story, "Life on Egypt Street" placed ninth in the Fourth International short story competition and was published in a collection entitled *The Time Collection*. The literary journal *Persimmon Tree* published a chapter of her memoir entitled "Under the Azure Greek Sky." Her work has appeared in the following journals: *The Hellenic Voice, Assay, The Raven's Perch, The Blue Nib, The Writers and*

Readers Magazine, and *The South Seattle Emerald.* She is currently working on poetry and a new novella, and is author of *Return to Thessaloniki/ Επιστροφή Στη Θεσσαλονίκη* released in the Greek language by Tyrfi Press. She has also published in English under the title *Sophia's Return: Uncovering My Mother's* Past by She Writes Press. Her novella, *An Unexpected Ally,* is forthcoming in the Fall of 2023. Visit her on Twitter: @kouidou Facebook: www.facebook.com/Kouidou/ Website: https:// sophiakouidougiles.com

Gerri Leen lives in Northern Virginia and originally hails from Seattle. In addition to being an avid reader, she's passionate about horse racing, tea, and collecting encaustic art and raku pottery. She has work appearing or accepted by *The Magazine of Fantasy and Science Fiction, Nature, Strange Horizons, Galaxy's Edge, Dark Matter, Daily Science Fiction*, and others. She's edited several anthologies for independent presses, is finishing some longer projects, and is a member of SFWA and HWA. See more at gerrileen.com.

A lover of all things chocolate, **John Muro** is a resident of Connecticut and a graduate of Trinity College, Wesleyan University, and the University of Connecticut. A two-time, 2021 nominee for the Pushcart Prize, John's poems have appeared or are forthcoming in numerous literary journals and anthologies, including *Barnstorm, Grey Sparrow, Mobius, Penumbra, River Heron, Sky Island* and the *French Literary Review. In the Lilac Hour*, John's first volume of poems, was published in 2020 by Antrim House, and his second volume, *Pastoral Suite,* will be released this spring. You can contact John on Instagram @johntmuro

John "Apollonius" Opsopaus, PhD has practiced magic, divination, and Neopaganism since the 1960s. He has some fifty publications in various magical and Neopagan magazines. He designed the Pythagorean Tarot and wrote the comprehensive *Guide to the Pythagorean Tarot* (Llewellyn, 2001). His *Oracles of Apollo* (Llewellyn, 2017) teaches divination based on ancient texts that he has translated, and his *Secret Texts of Hellenic Polytheism* (Llewellyn, 2022) presents the Neopagan religion of George Gemistos Plethon for modern practitioners. Opsopaus frequently presents workshops on Hellenic magic and Neopaganism, Pythagorean theurgy, divination, and related topics. In the early 1990s he founded the Omphalos, a networking organization for Neopagans in the Greek and Roman traditions and one of the first Internet resources for them. He is past coordinator of the Scholars Guild for the Church of All Worlds, past Arkhon of the Hellenic Kin of ADF (A Druid Fellowship), and a member of the Grey Council. His writings can be found at opsopaus.com.

Ariadne Rainbird writes: I am a psychologist, witch, pagan priestess and pagan prison chaplain, who has always felt a pull towards the Hellenic tradition. The Hellenic Gods have been with me since childhood, when I read the myths and tales of God and heroes as my bedtime reading, and they captured my imagination and my heart. I went on to study many different paths in adulthood, exploring Hinduism and Buddhism, the yogic path, training as a Priestess in the Fellowship of Isis, becoming initiated in a Wiccan coven and working with Welsh tradition Craft, exploring Druidry, studying the Norse tradition, but always returning to the Hellenic Gods, though often in an eclectic Wiccan way. Following having my daughter 21 years ago, and as a working single mum, finding running a coven no longer viable, I decided to follow my heart on a solitary path, learning more about the Hellenic Gods and more traditional ways of working with them. Eventually I discovered the Living Orphic tradition, and for the past few years I have been dedicated to that. I now have a small Orphic group and a website on the Orphic tradition. Previous published works include *Magick Without Peers*, a course in progressive witchcraft for the solitary practitioner, co-authored with David Rankine, and poetic and artwork contributions published in *First and Last: A Devotional for Hestia, At the Gates of Dawn and Dusk: A Devotional for Aurora, Eos and the Hesperides,*

Host of Many: Hades and His Retinue, and *Shield of Wisdom: A Devotional for Athena and Minerva,* and *With an Adamantine Sickle: A Devotional to the Titans.*

Rev. Donna M. Swindells writes: I walk the Mystic's path. A licensed Reverend, poet, and contributing writer, I am the founder of two schools within the Fellowship of Isis (The Iseum of Hathor, Lady of the West; and the Lyceum of Dionysus, Ariadne & Aphrodite, Star of the Sea). My background is in ancient Egyptian & Greek religion & Carmelite spirituality.

Suz Thackston is a solitary old witch and Hellenic priestess. She lives on little Moonshadow Farm with her nice husband, sweet dog, overbearing cats, fat mares, and a teeming host of spirits. She loves to wander in twilights and under the stars, murmuring to the trees, pouring libations, and tending to the needs of the beings, both solid and nebulous, who share the land with her. At some point she'll step into a pond or find herself inside a tree or wander into the mist and lose herself in Other. This is just as it should be.

Robin W. is an amateur poet, living in San Antonio, TX. They are a devotee of the Phrygian Great Mother of the Gods, and the Lord Áttis. Writing is how they connect with the Gods, and express devotion to Them. They run a small page called "For the Love of the Mother," on Facebook.

Ptolemy Soter, the first Makedonian ruler of Egypt, established the library at Alexandria to collect all of the world's learning in a single place. His scholars compiled definitive editions of the Classics, translated important foreign texts into Greek, and made monumental strides in science, mathematics, philosophy and literature. By some accounts over a million scrolls were housed in the famed library, and though it has long since perished due to the ravages of war, fire, and human ignorance, the image of this great institution has remained as a powerful inspiration down through the centuries.

To help promote the revival of traditional polytheistic religions we have launched a series of books dedicated to the ancient gods of Greece and Egypt. The library is a collaborative effort drawing on the combined resources of the different elements within the modern Hellenic and Kemetic communities, in the hope that we can come together to praise our gods and share our diverse understandings, experiences and approaches to the divine.

A list of our current and forthcoming titles can be found on the following page. For more information on the Bibliotheca, our submission requirements for upcoming devotionals, or to learn about our organization, please visit us at neosalexandria.org.

Sincerely,

The Editorial Board
of the Library of Neos Alexandria

Current Titles
Written in Wine: A Devotional Anthology for Dionysos
Dancing God: Poetry of Myths and Magicks
Goat Foot God
Longing for Wisdom: The Message of the Maxims
The Phillupic Hymns
Unbound: A Devotional Anthology for Artemis
Waters of Life: A Devotional Anthology for Isis and Serapis
Bearing Torches: A Devotional Anthology for Hekate
Queen of the Great Below: An Anthology in Honor of Ereshkigal
From Cave to Sky: A Devotional Anthology in Honor of Zeus
Out of Arcadia: A Devotional Anthology for Pan

Anointed: A Devotional Anthology for the Deities of the Near and Middle East

The Scribing Ibis: An Anthology of Pagan Fiction in Honor of Thoth

Queen of the Sacred Way: A Devotional Anthology in Honor of Persephone

Unto Herself: A Devotional Anthology for Independent Goddesses

The Shining Cities: An Anthology of Pagan Science Fiction

Guardian of the Road: A Devotional Anthology in Honor of Hermes

Harnessing Fire: A Devotional Anthology in Honor of Hephaestus

Beyond the Pillars: An Anthology of Pagan Fantasy

Queen of Olympos: A Devotional Anthology for Hera and Iuno

A Mantle of Stars: A Devotional Anthology in Honor of the Queen of Heaven

Crossing the River: An Anthology in Honor of Sacred Journeys

Ferryman of Souls: A Devotional for Charon

By Blood, Bone, and Blade: A Tribute to the Morrigan

Potnia: An Anthology in Honor of Demeter

The Queen of the Sky Who Rules Over All the Gods: A Devotional Anthology in Honor of Bast

From the Roaring Deep: A Devotional for Poseidon and the Spirits of the Sea

The Far-Shining One: A Devotional for the Spirits of the Sun

Ascendant II: Theology for Modern Polytheists

Circe's Cauldron: Pagan Poems and Tales of Magic and Witchcraft

The Host of Many: Hades and His Retinue

Shield of Wisdom: A Devotional for Athena and Minerva

Polytheistic Religion and Practice Volume One: Reflections and Essays

Among Satyrs and Nymphs: A Devotional Anthology to Hellenic Nature Spirits

With an Adamantine Sickle: A Devotional to the Titans

Forthcoming Titles

Lord of the Horizon: A Devotional in Honor of Horus

Of Sun and Earth and Eternity: A Devotional in Honor of Dragon and Serpent Deities

Lady of the Sycamore: A Devotional in Honor of Hathor

In a Shadow'd Mirror: Pagan Tales of Fantasy and Horror

BIBLIOTHECA ALEXANDRINA